THE
FACE
TO
FACE
BOOK

LEE A. STEED

WESTBOW·
PRESS
A DIVISION OF THOMAS NELSON
& ZONDERVAN

WestBow Press books may be ordered through booksellers or by contacting:

WestBow Press
A Division of Thomas Nelson & Zondervan
1663 Liberty Drive
Bloomington, IN 47403
www.westbowpress.com
1 (866) 928-1240

ISBN: 978-1-4908-8128-7 (sc)
ISBN: 978-1-4908-8129-4 (e)

Library of Congress Control Number: 2015908063

Print information available on the last page.

WestBow Press rev. date: 07/23/2015

You can choose today to be happy or not. Your circumstances really have nothing to do with it. The act being happy is still your choice. Though I may not be happy concerning the circumstances that surround me, I should not let that define whether I am happy or not.

"I am not saying this because I am in need, for I have learned to be content whatever the circumstances. I know what it is to be in need, and I know what it is to have plenty. I have learned the secret of being content in any and every situation, whether well fed or hungry, whether living in plenty or in want. I can do all this through him who gives me strength." (Philippians 3)

A quote from a very wise man.... Paul. Paul was in love with the same God, the same Savior as I am. I find myself falling short, getting distracted because of my circumstances and my wants. But I know the joy I feel when I focus my thoughts on Christ and his love for me.

> *How can He be the lion and the lamb?*
> *Easy, He is God. He is whatever you need him to be.*
> *Sometimes we need Him as the Lion.*
> *Sometimes we need Him as the Lamb.*

Everyday is a race. You can choose to sprint towards the finish line or you can choose a long distance run. Either way you will need set your pace. Endurance, Determination and Knowing where your goal is, are requirements. A sprinter rarely wins a long distance race, as does a long distance runner seldom win a sprint. Run the race that has been set before you. Don't envy the race of another. Don't compare your race to the one next to you. Only have hope that you will finish yours as a winner. It's a new day. Ready..... Set.....Go.....

I catch myself asking forgiveness for the same things. Asking for answers to the same questions. I find myself changing nothing, or very little, to reach new goals that I have set for myself. I catch myself seeing how close I can get, without crossing the line, one way or another. All I really want to see is shadows, not the true image. Why? Maybe because the true image lessens everything I thought I had done right. My best is nothing compared to the true image. It's easier to compare myself to the shadows. Why? Shadows don't have definite lines, but are blurred.

Christ came to clean up the blurred lines. To give me a true image. He came to fulfill every promise that was given thousands of years before and to bring new promises. To bring life to those of us that just go through the motions. My old prayers and my habitual sinning is making me motionless and lifeless. He has forgiven me of who I was. Now He wants to work through me doing His will. His desire for my life is the same as He has for yours. It's Heavenly. May Christ reveal himself to you today.

If you knew that today you were going to be robbed, what would you do? You would stay home and wait for the robber and get prepared to protect your belongings. Wouldn't you? You would fight to keep all the possessions that mean something to you or things you thought were worth fighting for. There is a thief coming. He could be in your home right now. He is worse than any other robber. He is after the one thing that is most precious... It's something he can't take from you but you must give it away. Your soul. This thief is subtle. He comes in with good meaning friends. Comes in with promises but leaves you in the worst condition possible.... Lost and hopeless. If you knew he was coming you would have been more prepared and ready for battle. Right? You have heard this all before and have grown tired of hearing it. So now.... You are vulnerable. It's not too late to prepare. Today is the day.

God's word is as alive today as it was the day it was written. Jesus loves you. He always has and He always will. Remember it won't be Satan that will send you to hell. It won't be Satan who will walk you to the very gates of eternal damnation. It will be the one that loved you enough to die for you that will take you to the doors of hell. Remember it was your choice, not His. Your will, not His. There is a narrow path and only those who are looking for it will find it. Keep seeking, keep knocking, keep asking.

Don't quit or give up on Christ because of the faults of those who claim to know him. Get to know Him yourself.

Why do you believe what you believe? Is it because someone told you what to believe? Or do you believe because you looked for the truth and found it for yourself

You can only go as far as the goal you have set. For some people just getting up in the morning is their greatest goal for the day. For others, they want to conquer the world. This time of year many people set goals. But how committed they are to attaining that goal is what makes the biggest difference between reaching their goal or not.

I'm not a good goal setter. I had this crazy thought that if I don't set one, I won't be disappointed. I was wrong. I was still disappointed. Disappointed about where I was in life. But that is exactly what I was aiming for. If you aim at nothing, that is exactly what you will hit.... nothing. If you have no aim, no goal, no commitment to anything then that is exactly what you will attain... an aimless, uncommitted life. Also known as an unhappy life.

It is never too late to change directions. It is never too late to aim, to set that goal, to become committed. That is the reason Christ came. God saw a bunch of aimless people heading in every wrong direction known to man and they thought they knew where they were going. They thought they were happy. Their small accomplishments disappeared amongst all their failures.

Jesus came to give us direction. To encourage us to set goals. To become committed people with a purpose. To encourage each other, to help each other, to walk together towards our goals in life. My main goal is Heaven. Then followed closely with encouraging as many people as possible to set the same goal. I don't want to just survive today, I want to win it. Ask and keep on asking. Knock and keep on knocking. Seek and keep on seeking.

Don't listen to what Satan says you are, remember he is a liar. If Jesus is your Savior, then...... you are redeemed.

I find myself falling short. Getting distracted by my circumstances and my wants. I've heard so much lately about how weak and unsuccessful the church as a whole is today. Sadly it isn't the church itself that is failing. It is the members. Not all of the members are sick and failing, but the majority is. We argue and disagree over things that Pharisees, Sadducees and Hypocrites fight over and they missed him. We treat the word of God as if it's a history lesson. As if it's for reading and entertainment. That it is a myth and trying to live it is wanting to live a fairytale life.

Few believers even know who their enemy is. (Hint, it isn't flesh and blood.) We talk more about what is wrong, and less about what each member needs to do personally to correct it. It is personal. But it is also not about fixing me only. It is also about me helping you to achieve your goal. It isn't about me understanding everything and having a complete knowledge of Him. It is about me helping you find Him. It isn't about my life being perfect before I can lead. It is about me helping you find the way to Him. My happiness doesn't come first, in fact yours does. It is what He talked and walked, isn't it?

What will it take to lead someone to Christ? Better yet what will it take for you to follow Him? I am not perfect. I will fail and I will fall. And when I do, I want to fall forward towards Him. If the church is weak, then I must become stronger and more faithful. If the church is failing, then I must try harder and put my failures behind me. If the church is full of sin, then I must stop sinning and let Jesus guide me. If I am a part of the church, I am a part of the problem. Start with me Lord. Start with me.

I've heard it said to "Treat others the way you want them to treat you." But what about this.... Treat others the way you want Jesus to treat you. If you forgive, you will be forgiven. if you give, then you will receive. If you receive, then you will give. It's how you live, what you do and how you do it. What you say and how you say it....etc.

This walk isn't just about how much knowledge I have. Otherwise those who cannot read or comprehend would never be able to understand him. It isn't only about what I see or feel. My God is so much more than a goose bump, a shiver, a ray of sunshine, a bolt of lightning or a clap of thunder. It is important to know who He really is.

It is also as important to know who the enemy is. (Once again, not flesh and blood.) He is a lot better at distracting me, judging me, putting me down and belittling me than anything or anyone else could ever be. He is also very good at making me think I am better, stronger, smarter than I am. And very good at convincing me that I am closer to God than anyone else. My enemy is extreme at times while at other times he is subtle and sneaky. My enemy will use those I love, those I don't like to be around, those I trust and those I don't, to turn my thoughts and actions a wrong direction. He will mask things as being good, when they are not. He will make things look bad when they are not. Satan is a liar and a thief. I know him. I know my God. I know who is greater.

God is doing something wonderful. Are you in or out? Be sure to weigh out your answer. Many have made quick decisions only to discover later they didn't understand the question. What God is doing involves more than you. It involves people you may not agree with and people who don't look like or act like you. It involves patience and endurance. It involves going through hard times and bad times and all the while not trying to offend other believers, but doing everything with a pure heart toward God. Constantly seeking His knowledge.

Sometimes by long suffering and sometimes by kindness. But always by the Holy Spirit, with a sincere love for others and the word of truth. All this with the power of God working in you. While you are holding on to the right things of God with both hands. You will be unknown by many but known by the creator. You will be punished possibly to the point of death. You may have sorrow upon sorrow, yet there will be a joy so deep it can never be taken. You will be enriching the lives of others, while owning nothing, yet having everything you need. Only a true man of God; only a true woman of God, could ever choose this life. There are no wimps, no self seeking people of God, only servants. Now once again, are you in or out?

Within my own strength, I can do little. With His Strength I can do everything. It's an everyday choice.... my strength or His.

A lot of churches are having financial difficulties. I have an idea.. What if during the week the church became a bar? What if the bar owner says he would pay a lot of money to rent the church building? What if they can guarantee everything would be spotless and the smell would be completely unnoticeable. They would take down all the bar decor, the beer ads, they would make sure the parking lot was in perfect order before they left on early Sunday morning. What if they said they would even put in a good word with their patrons to join us on Sunday? It would be good for their business and a good money maker for the church. Bills could be split and money could be made. How does that sound? Absurd? Why? The church is just a building made out of wood and stone, brick and mortar. It's just like any bar would be. It has everything that a good bar would love to have and to use. They could turn the music up and turn the lights down low. They could invite people to come and change the way they feel. They wouldn't make anyone feel like an outcast, but invited. Are you offended? Do you think it's the building that is holy? Some of you may be upset with this idea. Offended that I would suggest such a thing?

If that's the case, then why do you treat the true temple of God as if it's the devils den? Why do you allow the true temple of God to be infested with sin? Then on Sunday you try to clean it up, spray it with perfume, change your clothes and act like you love God. Why do you, not just allow, but invite sin in to your life to hang with you all week? Do you not know that God wants to dwell in you and not a building? Don't you know that the true temple of God sits between your own elbows? Don't you understand you are the temple of the Holy One and He wants to work through you. Not just on Sunday but all week long. Don't give Satan a moment of your time. Don't give him anything. Start this week cleaning out the filth you would not allow in church. Start acting like a temple ready to be used and blessed by God.

I would rather you be hot or be cold than to be just lukewarm. Because then at least you would recognize the difference. There is no place for lukewarm. There is no "just" getting by in the kingdom/family of God. Decide today where you stand. Remember there is no middle ground.

It's Sunday a perfect day to go to the big house and talk to the Master. It's been a tough week for so many. Are you tired? Are you weary? Life deals out things we don't expect. It's life. But there is a place you can go to get strength. Jesus.

Me without Christ.... been there, done that. Liked it, only for a while and then....... I really met Him. Now I know what mistakes are and the consequences that follow. Made too many. Ignored them and the regret didn't go away. Forgiveness from Him... was exactly what my soul needed. I got it. Now I'm free.

**We have a great cloud of witnesses watching us
Not just those who have gone on before us,
but those you work beside, live with, and meet every day.**

Jesus is alive!! Let's start living like we really believe that's true.

Ever wonder what the music would sound like if Mozart, Beethoven, or Chopin had the musical instruments we have today? Would they play quietly? No, I doubt it! What would happen if the disciples had the churches we have today, the safety we have, the finances, the education? Would they sit quietly? No! What if King David had the speakers and microphones that we have? Would he have left them silently inside the church? No!

Nothing would sound like it does today. Nothing would look like it does today. They were chosen for then you are chosen for now. I have heard too many say, there is nothing at the church for them anymore? Really? Did you really say that? There is plenty at the church to do. There are too many souls that need Christ. There are too many sick and dying that need help. There are too many people wandering aimlessly, needing someone to show the love of Christ to them. There are too many lonely, hurting people.....and that is just inside the church, let alone those who aren't a part of the church body (yet).

I am afraid of what Paul would say. I would tremble at what David would do. I would be ashamed, to let my Jesus see the ones He died for acting the way they act and calling themselves a believer and follower of Christ and say "There is nothing in the church for me." Sadly He does see it. Jesus may call you a hypocrite. Paul would tell you to grow up. The martyrs for Christ would not be easy on you with so much whining over menial things. Nothing for you? Are you wanting your name in lights? Are you wanting man's recognition or God's?

I am guilty of these things myself as well. Guilty of about not getting things my way. Just plain guilty. If we want the meat of God then let us put away our childish ways. Set down our bottle of milk and grab a fork and grow up. It isn't about you and it's not about me. It is about the Kingdom of God. His righteousness, His holiness, His pure love. May we who are called by His name, act like we are called. Do the things we are called to do and not just in the church, but outside the church walls. Time is short, His coming is soon. Had the owner of the house known when the robber was coming, he would have been ready. Let's fall in love with Jesus, and stand on his love. Jesus loves us. Let us remember that.

A farmer had two sons. One raised sheep and the other planted crops. Their father had taught both of them everything they knew. From tilling the land to tending to injured lambs. For as long as they could remember, they had taken their best and offered it to God. The day came to give. The older brother that planted grain, brought in some of his grain to offer to God. The younger brother that raised sheep, brought in the firstborn of his flock. God didn't accept the grain but accepted the firstborn of the flock. The older brother's feelings were hurt. God spoke to the older brother and asked him why he was so mad and why had his face changed?

Don't you know if you do your best you will be accepted? But if you don't, then regret sits just outside your door. Regret has a desire for you... to cause you pain. But you should rule over it. If you give God your best, no matter what your best is, he will accept it. But most of us just want to get by. Why? Funny how when we buy something that we pay hard earned money for, we want it to work. We want it to be the best. If it isn't then we get mad and return it. Or won't accept it. Why then would we want to give God something we wouldn't want and expect him to accept it? What is your best? Time, money, special skills, the ability to comfort or help someone, etc? No matter if your best seems least among men, God is pleased with it. Be blessed in knowing He loves you, He always has and always will.

Each day He teaches me more. Sometimes it sounds like thunder and sometimes it sounds like rain. Sometimes there is no sound at all.... But knowing He is here.... gives me strength for today, hope for tomorrow and security for my future.

Most conversations start with a question..... How are you?..... How are you doing?......What have you been up to?....Etc. This conversation started with a question as well. The starter of the conversation had a plan, and that plan was to manipulate, twist, and lie. He was strategic in his first question, because he knew if he could get the conversation started then he could manipulate it. He could deceive the one he was speaking to. And it worked. He asked her a question, "You can't eat from any of the trees here can you?" She replied, trying to set the record straight, entering into the conversation, "Yes, I can, I can eat of any of the trees here, just not that one." One rule was given. Do not touch, do not eat of that tree. The penalty was death. His cunning question stirred her want to correct him, to enter into a conversation with him. Once it was started, he had her attention. Satan is very good at getting us into a conversation with Him. He will tell a partial truth, just to get you to correct him. But it's the reply that gets it started. Next time he wants your time or tells you a partial truth. The next time he tries to cause doubt in your promise... ignore him. Don't enter into a conversation with him. Don't reply. Just delete. He can talk, but you don't have to listen.

Everyone has mountains. Satan took Jesus to the top of a very high mountain and told him he would give Jesus everything if he would bow down to him. Jesus spoke and said there is only one God and you are not him. I serve only one God and I will bow only to Him. (My paraphrasing). Maybe the reason we have trouble with our mountains is because we tend to bow to the wrong god or gods. We can't serve them and a Heavenly God. So just what is your mountain anyway? Is it one you have built yourself? Is it one that Satan placed there to stop you or slow you down? Is it a mountain God wants you to climb for wisdom and endurance? Once you determine what your mountain is, you can speak to it, climb it, or go around it. Remember, it's your mountain.

Don't give up today. You don't know what tomorrow may bring. Where there is faith, there is hope. My hope for tomorrow is not determined by my circumstances of today. Remember, Jesus really does love you.....

I asked God "where I should begin reading?" "The beginning" He replied. It has been more than my mind can comprehend, how "the beginning happened". God spoke, and all of heaven was created. He spoke and light appeared. He spoke and the waters were separated. He spoke it all into existence. There was one thing He formed. There was one creation that wasn't spoken into existence... man. Man was created by the hand of God. Formed out of the dust of the earth. Then God breathed the breath of life into this marvelous creation. Why was this creation so different? Why was this life so special? Formed into the image of God? I'm not sure that it was a physical resemblance, but a spiritual resemblance. A spiritual being created for the one purpose of having a relationship with a spiritual God. Isn't it amazing? Think about it. You were born to have a relationship with God. To walk with Him, to share your life with Him. Yet many of us treat this relationship like we treat all the others in our life. This relationship was so special to Him, that He sent His only Son to this earth to restore it. This relationship is so important to Him that Jesus died for it. He gave it all. How can I ignore such a special relationship with Him? How can I take it for granted each day?

God is faithful to keep His promises. God is able to hear and to answer your prayers. But are you praying? Then keep praying. Are you continuing to stand on His promises? Then keep standing. Or have you forgotten because life has gotten you too busy? Remember He really does love you. Don't judge his love by the kind of love this world offers. His love is so much more.

I've always heard a one sided relationship never works, but it seems that's what I seem to give God. It amazes me, that He, the creator of all things could want a relationship with someone who is as broken as me, but He does. He wants a relationship with you and me. With everyone. I don't want to ignore Him today. I want to walk with Him and talk with Him throughout my day. Whether I am at work, at home, with family and friends or all alone. My sole(soul) purpose is searching for Him. If I seek Him, I will find Him. If I knock, He will open it. If I ask, He will answer.

Almost every life lived has left a memory. Whether it is good or bad. It is up to the living to decide which direction they will remember and follow. I love reading this book that encourages me and warns me of actions taken by people who lived before me. Examples of how to live my life or how not to live it. Examples of extreme giving and extreme selfishness. Examples of things worth fighting for and things that are not. Though the bible was written a long time ago, it is still just as true today as the days and times it was written. There has been nothing new to come up today that didn't come up then. The same battles over the same things. I have read of the victories of those doing the right things and read of the complete destruction of those who did not do the right things. This book will guide me, if I let it. It will encourage me and warn me, if I pay attention. It will lead me to success if I follow it. It isn't just the words that capture my attention, but it's the spirit by which it was written. My eyes will never see some of the places I have read about. My ears may never hear the sounds of walls falling. But this I know... the promises that were given then, are the same today. This book has lead many a soul through troubled times. It has lead them to Him. He is above all things. He is greater than all things. He is the great.... I AM.

God *didn't promise life would be easy.*
He did promise He would walk with you every step.

If you look for mercy you will find it. If you look for revenge, you will find that too. If you keep knocking on the door of regrets, you will find yourself in the company of many. If you seek for the good things of God, you will surely see them. What you are really looking for you will find. Whichever door you are truly knocking on, will be opened up to you. What you are honestly asking for, you will receive. Be careful what you ask for. Be wise about what you are seeking. Be cautious what doors you knock on. Not all things are good and not all things are Godly. Do all that you do as if you are doing it for our Lord.

My most frustrating moments are having something to say and not being able to say them. I think of the words but sometimes I just can't put them together quick enough. But it is teaching me and slowly I am learning. My tongue can bring life or death to many situations and circumstances. It can bring discontentment, division, bitterness and hatred. My tongue is the most abusive member of my body. But He was led to slaughter, knowing the truth and He never spoke a word. Remember the saying, "Sticks and stones may break my bones, but words will never hurt me"? It is a lie. I would rather be hit with a stick or stone than hear a bad word spoken about someone I love. Remember.....slow to speak.... and slow to anger.

It's one of those mornings that music seems to touch my soul. We all have a hungry soul. Be careful what you feed it. If you feed it anger, then anger will grow. If you feed your soul sadness, then sadness will grow. If you feed your soul lies, then lies will grow. If you feed your soul love, then love will grow. But if you feed your soul the truth of God's word, then everything will grow. Anger towards sin, sadness towards the lost, love and compassion towards those around you and a passion for our Lord and Savior Jesus Christ.

Some will use the Word of God for wrong reasons and will not walk in the power of it. But those who walk upright before the Lord will walk in its power, its peace, with wisdom and understanding. It is a blessing to those who believe and is useless to those who do not.

Keeping anything between you and God? If so you have an idol, another god between you and Him. The Holy God of Heaven wants all of your attention, not leftovers.

So far in my life there is one thing that makes me special. Maybe not to you, maybe not to them..... but to Him. I've given my life to Him, my heart. It hasn't been easy, nor was it suppose to be (as some suppose). I've weighed it out and I continue to weigh it out daily. My life as how it used to be compared to how my life will be. My future wins hands down. I don't have the best of everything but I don't want the best. He will meet and provide every desire of my heart.

I've made too many mistakes thinking I had to meet up to the standards of others. But I found the easiest standard to really meet up to is His. How? How is His standard easier? He helps me, guides me, shows me, and provides for me. They judge me, criticize me, manipulate and dishonor me. I love Him, and best yet, He loves me. No one can beat that. Nope, no one. I love my family and my friends and I pray for them. Just think, someone could be mentioning your name to the Creator of all things. Asking for your protection and your guidance towards Him. I am praying for the day, you make Him your best friend. Your BFF. Loving God and loving you.

It seems to be relentless. So many needs. So many lost. So many sick. So many things coming at us from so many directions. How overwhelmed many of us have become, believers or not. If the one we are to imitate withdrew from people to pray, then that is what we are supposed to do as well. When Jesus left for the wilderness, the mountain, the garden, He left the needs behind him. Not because He didn't want to deal with them, like I want to do. He left them to get more strength and wisdom from His Heavenly Father to deal with them when He returned.

I use the phrase "I'll be praying for you" too easily. It seems to be more of a greeting. Even those who rarely talk to God and don't have a relationship with him use it. How am I any different than a non believer? Sometimes I do pray when I say it. Sometimes I don't. That is unacceptable, don't you think? Prayer gives us wings, power, wisdom, etc. Take time today and really pray. If you have walked away from Him, get your heart right with God and pray. Situations and circumstances are distracting us from the call on our lives, prayer and spending time with God is the best thing to do when you need to refocus.

What is it going to take to get your attention? What is it going to take to get you to believe? Really believe? I've gone to church almost all of my life. It never made me a believer. Attending church makes you a believer just as much as going to a basketball game sitting in the stands makes you a basketball player. What does it take to be a basketball player or a football player? Any kind of player? You have to be in the game. If you aren't in the game, you are sitting in the stands. You are just watching the game, screaming how unfair things are, telling players what to do and how to do it. You're the one who just dreams of doing something, but never trying.

To the player....the feeling you have when you are in the zone, the game is different isn't it. You don't hear the crowd, but you feel them and it drives you to do more, try harder. The fact that you are ahead or behind doesn't even enter your thoughts. It's the rush, the adrenaline that moves you. It is your passion for the game that drives you, the desire to win. You can hear your coach calling out the play. You can hear your team mates calling out to you from the bench. Being a believer in Jesus is a lot like that.

Those who are in the game are driven with passion, a passion for a Savior. This passion can make the scariest moments in life seem to disappear, because you are in the "zone", the presence of the One true God. You can't hear the crowds screaming at you, but you feel them, you can hear your coach and those sitting on the bench calling your name, calling out the play.... Paul and the disciples, Mary, Martha, Stephen, martyr's of Christ. The coach is awesome, He knows the right plays, He knows what the other team is about to do. He gives you the play... Now what? Are you sitting in the stands, grumbling and complaining or are you in the game? You can't do anything sitting, except watch. Get up and get in the game. Find out if you really are a believer. Find out if you even want to play. Life really isn't a game of win some, lose some. Jesus doesn't want to lose but it isn't His decision, it is yours. You decide.......Want to play?

The days I don't hear His voice, are the days I'm suppose to have faith and trust Him more. Having faith in something you can see, isn't faith at all.

I love the parables. Each time I read them I get just a little more understanding of Him. There is so much more to them than what you see. I believe inside of us is a garden. This garden has so many wonderful things. But then comes sin, and here comes life. Worrying about life has caused me to pace back and forth creating hard places and paths. Concerns about bills and health, life and death has caused weeds to grow. Temptations has caused rocks of sin to suddenly show up. My beautiful garden isn't so pretty anymore.

The small area that is still growing, it has some fruit, but it is barely enough to sustain my life. The rocks and weeds and paths just keep growing. Suddenly I decide to start tending my garden. I get my hoe. I get my shovel. I get my gloves and I get to work. Get rid of those worries. Throw out those sins. Soften those hard places. So much work to do, it is overwhelming. Some rocks are too big. Some weeds go too deep and some of these paths seem to be made of stone. I can't tend this garden on my own. I need professional help. I call to Him and He comes. He comes because I am willing to give my garden to him. The rocks I can't move, He moves easily. The weeds that have roots so deep, are nothing for Him to pull. The paths that have been trodden so long, turn to powder in His hands.

But then I show Him my good soil, my small plot that I have been taking care of. It's my trophy. "Look" I say, "how beautiful it is. See my fruit?" He smiles at me, and says "I can make it better. Let's spread seed over the rest of your garden." I reply that I can't take care of anything bigger. It would be more than I could handle on my own. "I see" He says. "Your happy just being sustained, but not living?" That's when I begin to understand. He didn't come just to help me get my garden under control, He came to help me take my garden back, to increase me, to stretch me. He says He will help me every day that I ask Him to. I can trust Him or I can choose to continue to do this on my own. He can increase my garden from barely supporting me to supporting many others as well.

You see He wants me to share my garden. To give starts of it to others so they can get their garden growing too. I have always shared with others... my weeds, my rocks, my paths, and a little of my fruit. He wants me to share more fruit and get rid of the rest. It will take work, time and sacrifice. It will cause me pain and leave me with greater endurance. He won't leave me to do it alone. Nor will He leave you. Here is Jesus. Here is your start.

I don't have your answer. But I know who does. Jesus. He alone understands. He alone can change your life. You've searched everywhere only to find it all empty promises. You've tried all you know to try, yet you keep having the same problems. You may have heard about Christianity, but most of the Christian's you know are fake. I can apologize for only me. I am sorry that I have been so misleading. My life is not perfect. I fail a lot. I mess up my life by stupid decisions too. I am not as different from you as I think I am. I need forgiveness as much as you do. Not from you, but from Jesus Christ. I have represented him wrongly. I have cheapened

His gospel. I have downgraded His requirements. I have failed Him with my wrong choices. But I choose this day to try harder, with His help, because on my own I am unable to do it. Neither can you. All we have to do is talk to Him and then listen and obey.

We've all been complaining about winter. But a silly thought crossed my mind. December 21 began winter and is suppose to last until March 21. We have dates that was set by man, and the last date isn't too far away. But God put the seasons in place. As much as I don't like being cold, it makes me think. You can't rush what God is doing. We have been so used to mild winters that now when a hard winter hits, all we do is complain. Sick of snow. Sick of cold. Sick of being sick.. etc. I've said it myself.

But remember, we can't rush God. We can't push Him and we can't make Him. All we can do is ask Him. Ask Him for the strength to endure the rest of the days of winter. And when the first sign of spring is here, the snow melts from the ground and the weather warms up, I will praise the Lord. When the temperatures get hot, the swimming pool is warm and there isn't enough ice to cool my drink....... even then I will praise the Lord. Maybe it's just time to praise Him. God is worthy.

Jesus loves you and He likes what He sees...... not because of what you have done, but because of what He did. You can't pay him back, you can't be good enough, you can't give enough, read enough, pray enough.... Stop condemning yourself. Are you trying? Really, are you putting in the effort? He sees it, yes He does. He loves your hard effort to please Him. He loves the fact that you are trying. But even better than that, He wants to help you, to become everything He sees in you. Remember, Jesus loves you.

Such a gorgeous morning. We aren't guaranteed to see every sunset. But those who love the Lord will be overwhelmed at the sight of the sunrise. May your day be blessed. May you find peace in every circumstance, joy in every sorrow. May you know that He is Lord and Savior. May your heart be filled with love and your eyes filled with hope. Remember to stand on the rock, when you find yourself surrounded by sinking sand.

Ok, you are stuck at home. Turn the TV off. Put the phone down and read. Preferably Gods Word. Yeah, there are books that are hard to read in it, but every word was written for you. Every story told was told for you. Every blessing and every curse. Gods goodness doesn't outweigh his wrath. They are equal.

I guess I'm a little emotional today. Missing those who have gone on before me. I am reminded of those who have fought for us and those who are fighting for us now. There are some who don't believe it's right to fight. Those who believe it is best to let things go, let things be. "It's freedom" they say. "It is their right" they say. Many try to destroy our freedom and without men and women willing to fight for it, we will lose our freedom. Not just any freedom, but mine and yours.

Right now I am free to tell you what I believe in and who I believe in. But there are those that would call me a religious tyrant, because I believe the Word of God. For many years we have given up our rights. They haven't been taken away. The right to call sin, just what it is,... sin. Men and women have died to give us freedom of speech, freedom to worship, freedom to bear arms and many other freedoms.

There have also been men and women who have given up their lives so we can continue sharing the truth. The truth of Jesus Christ. His death has always meant more to those that understood it. Just like our military men and women's deaths will always mean more when we understand why they did it and who they did it for. Love God and love your country. Pray to God for his mercy and his grace and pray for our country that we will turn from our wicked ways and be healed. Thank a soldier. You don't know what they have been through or are still going through, just so I could write this and you could read it.

"I love you," is sometimes a cliché that so many use without ever understanding it's true meaning. "I love you" is so much more. It is a sacrifice. It means giving when you have nothing left to give. It isn't getting what you want when you want it. Jesus asks us to follow Him. To pick up our lives and follow Him. For many of us we will have to leave our lives behind in order to follow Him. Are you ready to answer? Are you ready to follow Him?

The sins we commit do not go unnoticed by a Holy God. They are not pushed aside, because "He loves you". Once a broken heart asks for forgiveness, it is forgiven. Sadly we go to him more because we are "caught in sin", not because we feel guilty of it.

It's Friday and God is good. He is for you, not against you. Unless of course you are His enemy. If you are not for God, then you are against Him. Which is not a good place to be. God isn't that hard to please. Obey Him and His Word. Love Him by putting Him first in everything. Then live your life as His child, doing what is right. Even if it doesn't make you popular.

Sometimes all that lies between me and falling apart is a song. A song can lift my spirits, calm my uneasy soul, it can encourage me when nothing else can, it can fill my mind with precious memories, it can do some pretty amazing things. Just a note, a tune and then there I go. My life is filled with songs. A song my grandmother sang in church, a song my mom would sing about her heavenly home, my dad singing with my little church quartet, songs my mother in law still sings and songs my husband sings. For me there is a special spirit that dwells within the melodies of a song. Precious Memories, This is My Story, There's a Mansion just over the Hilltop, God on the Mountain, Arise my Love. 10,000 Reasons. Redeemed. Now doesn't that just start the memories, doesn't it just stir your spirit, encourage your weary soul?

Does this sound familiar? *"Take a good, hard look at your life. Think it over. You have spent a lot of money, but you haven't much to show for it. You keep filling your plates, but you never get filled up. You keep drinking and drinking and drinking, but you're always thirsty. You put on layer after layer of clothes, but you can't get warm. And the people who work for you, what are they getting out of it? Not much— a leaky, rusted-out bucket, that's what."* God said that in the Old Testament. It means the same thing for today!! That's why God said *"Take a good, hard look at your life. Think it over."* Are you looking over your life? If you have you may be at loss for what to do. Here is your answer. *"Here's what I want you to do: Climb into the hills and cut some timber. Bring it down and rebuild the Temple. (You've got to work at it, you've got to work for the right reason). Do it just for me. Honor me. You've had great ambitions for yourselves, but nothing has come of it. The little you have brought to my Temple I've blown away—there was nothing to it. "Because while you've run around, caught up with taking care of your own houses, my Home is in ruins. That's why. Because of your stinginess. And so I've given you a dry summer and a skimpy crop. I have matched your tight-fisted stinginess by decreeing a season of drought, drying up fields and hills, withering gardens and orchards, stunting vegetables and fruit. (Isn't that scary? God can and will match our stinginess). Nothing—not man or woman, not animal or crop—is going to thrive."* (Haggai 1:9-11 The Message)

You have left my house in ruins. You've been walking in a fake sense of spirituality. Your heart is nowhere close to Him. Your thoughts are on yourself... what you can get and what you want. Not on what He wants for you. What should you do? LISTEN! That's what you do. You stop and listen. "...Then all the people with them listened, really listened, to the voice of their God. When God sent the prophet Haggai to them, they paid attention to him. In listening to Haggai, they honored God. Then Haggai, God 's messenger, preached God 's Message to the people: "I am with you!" God 's Word. This is how God got all the people moving— got them working on the Temple.... (Haggai 1:12-14 The Message).

Honor God and remember the temple of today is you!! Living a life worthy of his blessings takes time and work. But remember He doesn't wait for you to fail. He waits for you to succeed in rebuilding his temple. Not the building, but you, the true temple of God.

The love of Christ. Who can explain it? Many have felt it. Many have lost their lives because of it. Yet they live. Narrow is the path that leads to life, and few find it. Wide is the path that leads to death and it is open wide for anyone to enter. If you aren't seeking for the narrow path, then you will find yourself on the wide one.

There are only two paths, not three. There are many on the wide path, walking back and forth having a good time. At first they are enjoying life, living the way they want to live. Living it up, they say. But then they find that they are afraid and begin pacing back and forth. Anxious, because the path they are on isn't fun anymore. They are trapped. lost and hurting. The others passing by, don't even see them now. When it was a fun path, they had lots of friends. They were "living it up". But when the fun left, so did all their friends. There is no one that can save you, except The One. The One that called out your name the day you started on the wrong path. He walked that path many years ago, not as one who was on a mission to have "fun", but The One who was on a mission to "Save".

He led many from that place and will continue to rescue some at the gate. The narrow path is covered. It isn't easy to walk on. It requires special armor due to its difficulty, and it gets so dark you need a lamp to follow it. This lamp doesn't run on fuel or batteries. This lamp is the Word of God. The path will only light up, when the lamp is used. There aren't many walking on it. But you can see where others have gone on before you. At times you may begin to feel lonely, but remember, you have your armor and your lamp. You have read about the place this path leads, yet wonder why it is so difficult to get there. You've even thought a time or two, of going back. But the lamp, it just keeps shining.

At the end of both paths there are gates. One gate is small, the other is giant. One gate offers true happiness, and the other, well, it offers hell. You will have no friends, no family, nothing in hell. It wasn't meant for you. It wasn't meant for any human. It was designed to torture for all eternity Satan, and his fallen angels. Heaven is filled with those that endured the narrow path and walked through the narrow gate. There are wonders and unexplainable feelings of love. Both places were created by the same creator. As magnificent as Heaven is, Hell is just as horrific. Heaven is filled with singing, hell is filled with screaming. Choose wisely the path you follow. Every step is your choice.

There are two that are searching the earth today.
God is looking for someone to be strong in.
Satan is looking for someone to destroy.
Which one will choose you today? Don't assume anything.
Be sure your heart is right with God
or you will be accessible to the other.

It isn't what goes into your body that ruins your integrity, it is what comes out of you. Adversity will bring out the worst or the best in you. The choice is always yours.

Trust Him. He has a lot more experience than you do. He was here in the beginning and He will be there when it's all over.

Faith in humanity has tainted our faith in God. Many compare the faithfulness of God to the unfaithfulness of people. God is always faithful. He is always fair. He is always just. He is always right.

Ring, ring. He's here? Really? Where? Thanks, I've been looking for Him for over a month. I'll see you tomorrow at church, Ok? Bye. He's here. He is really here in my town. He is on the other side of town. (Minutes later) There he is. I jump out of the car and I run to Him. Barely catching my breath, I ask Him the one question that I have been desperately wanting to find the answer to. "Jesus, What am I supposed to do to get eternal life".... His reply wasn't exactly what I was looking for. He says, "You know the commandments. Do them." It stops me in my tracks. I gasp, then reply "But Jesus, I have done those since I was young. What else is there? What great thing do you want me to do now?" His reply again isn't what I wanted to hear. He looks at me with such love and patience and says, "Then sell everything that is keeping you here and come with me." Shocked and bewildered I just stand there. Everything I have? But it all means so much to me. I have worked hard for it. I have spent countless hours working, just to get it. He knows I love Him and I can tell by the look in His eyes, that He really wants me to come with Him. But, can I sell everything? Am I even willing to sell it all? That isn't what I thought He would say that I was good, that I have done enough. I thought He might even say, I need you to be a teacher, a preacher, one of my apostles. But not sell everything. My heart breaks, as I realize, I do not love Him like that. I turn and walk away with tears running down my cheeks. I hear Him mention, as I walk away, how hard the road is that leads to heaven. Even those who were with Him, were startled. As Jesus leads them further down the road, I notice that those close to Him are still amazed, but those that follow further behind, were afraid. So I wonder.... do they too, have things that they want to hold on to? Do they also have things that mean more to them, than He did. Is that what slows their steps and puts fear in their hearts? Do we own the things we have or do the things we have, own us? If we just own something, we are more willing to get rid of it. But if it owns us, it holds on to us. Our love of possessions, our things, has gotten many of us into trouble, financially, spiritually and emotionally. They are things that make us "happy". But in God's eyes, they are unwanted and unneeded baggage holding us back from completely, following Him. The road to heaven isn't easy. In fact, it's impossible for us to walk alone. But with God all things are possible.

He is God. We are not.

Why is it so hard to remember that Jesus is in the boat? Just like the disciples we tend to panic and even get mad at Him. Remember, He got in the boat with us at the beginning and He won't get out until it's over.

It's easy to let life and it's circumstances define who you are. But that is not who you are. God says you are so much more. Let God define you and share with you who you are and who you could be in Him. If you are forgiven, then you are Redeemed. If not, then you are lost. Let the love of Christ find you and change you.

You can do it, start with just one breath, one step at a time. You will never climb that mountain until you take that first step. God's grace is enough to take you the rest of the way.

Don't just read, but read slowly and listen to what His word is saying. Let it sink in. Yes, God's word is alive. If your soul is weak and dying....... give it life.

I love the parables. Each time I read them, another door is opened, another part is revealed of how GREAT my God is. Wheat and the Tares. There will always be someone ready to destroy every good thing in you. Yeast and the Flour, your attitude will spread. Whether it's a good attitude or a bad one. So what can we learn from a simple parables?....... a lot. Where there is good, bad isn't far away. A bad attitude is just as contagious as a smile. And those are just two of many parables. So it comes down to this, it's my choice. Being a servant is a choice. Being a jerk is a choice. Today I choose to serve Him. So, how do I do that? By loving those around me. Some are a lot easier to love than others, this is true. I'm just glad God chose to love me anyway. And because He loves me anyway, it shows me how I can love others. His way is perfect. His will is different than mine and it's better. I know I don't like His will for my life sometimes, because His will is that I grow in Him and growing hurts. Growing involves pruning, replanting and time. Growing involves the dying of myself. Of which, none of it I enjoy. But He is always faithful to me. The Sower parable is my very favorite. Those who have ears, listen to what the spirit says. Those who aren't listening, just enjoy the story.

They called for him when she was at deaths door. "I'm on my way" He said. So He began the journey. When He arrived they told him He was too late, she was dead. He disagreed with them. "No she is only sleeping" He said. Many of us believe it is too late to receive our promises. We believe the promise is dead. When Jesus gives a promise, He is never late and it is never dead. Some of our promises may be only sleeping. Just waiting for the day our Savior walks in and speaks life back into it. Stop mourning the suspected loss of a promise. If God gave it, He will complete it. He didn't promise all our troubles would disappear if we followed Him. He did promise He wouldn't let us go through any of them alone.

He said it would happen and it did. He said I would deny him and I did. But He also said He would rise again and He did that too. Jesus is alive. There is no need to fear death unless of course you don't have a good relationship with the Savior.

How long would it take to fill the ocean if all you had was a teaspoon of water? Great things are impossible without God. Jesus filled the belly of 5,000+ people with only a small amount of food. He is the only one who can fill the ocean with a teaspoon of water. What is impossible with man has always been possible with God. So don't quit believing for your promise. Don't lose faith in God. Stir up the joy that He placed in you. Ask for peace and endurance to carry you through. Look for God in the craziest places. He lives in more than a building built by men.

I can't do anything right. Everything I do just falls apart and accomplishes nothing when I do it on my own. Except loving Jesus. I cannot love Him for you. You must love Him yourself.

All I know is once I was blind, but now I see. God is good and He is full of justice. I deserve a terrible life, but He has promised an eternal one. He is my hope for today and tomorrow.

I have the blood stains on my own hands. My hands were involved in that terrible day. No one put it there. I, yes I did it. I am guilty of denying my Lord. I am guilty of killing Him. Yet He loved me enough to die willingly. He washed away my evil deeds and He remembers them no more. But not you. You remember my past. You remember my faults and accuse me. But you aren't the one I serve anymore. He is and Jesus is the one that matters.

I love my Jesus and He loves me. He has asked me to invite you to come to His house today. I know He will be so happy if you come. I know if you decline his invitation He will be terribly disappointed and then I will be asked to go and invite others. His table is spread with the most amazing things and He is planning on a lot of you coming to His feast. Sadly though I was turned down by many of those that had better things to do. "It's such a pretty day", they said. "It's my only day to do what I want to do, maybe next time I will come." Those words broke my heart. You see, these were my friends. These were my loved ones. These were the ones I had been in His house before with and I knew He wouldn't be happy. Just as I thought, He is sending me out again to invite all the people I don't know. To invite those that He hasn't met, those that are filthy with sin. They were more than willing to stop what they were doing and come to His dinner. They were all given new clothes, a clean soul, and were completely forgiven of everything. They thoroughly enjoyed the wonderful meal you were invited to. It is always a good thing to see my Jesus enjoy those that really love Him. During dinner a few of my friends tried to join us, but the doors were shut and their name was not on the list to enter.

"Maybe next time", they said. Maybe there isn't a next time, maybe this was the last. Please don't wait. Dinner is served and He won't wait for you forever.

If there is one thing that I would like to say to you today, it is..... Hold on. Don't give up. Hold on to the hand of the One who loves you. Don't give up on the One who gave it all, just so you would have a chance. Every morning, each night, every minute Jesus waits. Not just for me, but for you. He won't let go. He isn't like so many who have left you, failed you, forgotten you. Jesus can't...... He promised. So before you go any further..... just call out His name. Jesus, is as close as a whisper.

When all else fails, stand. Praise The Lord for the things He has done. Praise him for the things he is going to do. Praise him for the good and praise him for the not so good. At all times, praise The Lord. Then you will feel His strength. Then you will feel His peace and his power. But do all that you can and then stand.

Life proven rule. If you plant corn you will get corn. If you plant wheat you will get wheat. If you plant hatefulness, you will receive hatefulness. If you plant love, you will get love. Get the picture?

I sent out a dove this morning and it brought back a leaf. So the storm is over. Now to clean up my ark.

God is not dead. He would love a visit from you today.

A farmer had a large field. When he received his seed, he planted sparingly. He didn't plant any on the pathways. None even close to the rocks and he planted no seed where there were any weeds. At the time of harvest what do you think he harvested? Another farmer had a small field, he received his seed and he planted seed everywhere. He planted on the pathways. He planted among the rocks. He planted seed even where the weeds were. He left no soil uncovered by his seed. At the time of harvest what do you think he harvested? Both farmers received the same sunshine, the same rain. Yet only one had a great harvest. Jesus has given you something to share, so share it. Some will not receive it. Some will receive it with joy and then fall away. While other's will receive it and grow, but let things of life choke it out. But there will be one who will receive it and share it with others. Remember it's not up to you to only share it in good places, but also in bad places. It's up to God to make it grow. You don't always know the condition of the heart that is about to receive it, but God does.

Are you looking at your situation? Is it too big? Is it overwhelming? I've been there and I fight most days not to go back. Is your situation, your circumstance, your dreams, your wants, your desires, are they your idol? Is your plan, your family, your job, your home, are they your idol? What is standing between you and God? Pride? Bitterness? Reputation? Finances? What is it? On God's side there is nothing. There is no depth, no width, no height that can separate God from you. There is no principality, no power, no ruler, no government that can separate God from you. There is no man, no woman, no evil thing, no earthly thing that can separate God from you. There is no bill, no dollar, no collection agency, no job or lack of employment, that can separate God from you. There is no prison, no home, no chain and no freedom, that can separate God from you. There is nothing that can separate Him from you. Now, what is on your side? What have you put there? Remove it and put it where it belongs, below Him. He is waiting to be the Number 1 thing in your life. Not the option.

If you keep looking back and holding on to your successes or failures, you may never reach the goal Christ has for your life.

Be a good example of Christ. Don't worry about what people might think or what people might say about you. Who are you trying to please anyway? Them or God? Let your conduct be worthy of the good news of Jesus Christ. Don't let your life tarnish what others (who don't believe) think about Christ. Don't let your actions indicate that His forgiveness and His salvation doesn't change you. That your claim to follow Him is no different than who they are already following. Don't let your actions and your attitude be the same as someone who doesn't believe. Let Christ be Christ in you.

God's grace is as deep as your sins. God's grace is as deep as my own sins. The more sin the more grace? That doesn't mean to go and sin. It means no matter your sin, His grace is sufficient. It is 100% forgivable. Without His grace you walk in mercy. You walk in your sin, you take great pleasure in your sin. But He loves you enough to give you one more chance to make it right between you and Him.

My Savior Jesus is mine. Living He loved me. Dying He saved me. Rising He justified me. I'll love Him forever more.

I know whom I have believed and I am persuaded that He is able to keep that which I have committed unto Him against that day. Today my daughter was in an accident. She is fine. Damage to the car turned out to be minimal. She was protected, not lucky. I have committed my children to the Lord. Once again He proved to me.... He's got this all under control.

I liked this story and thought I would share it. It is not mine. Francis of Assisi once invited an apprentice to go with him to a nearby village to preach. The young monk quickly agreed, seizing an opportunity to hear his teacher speak. When they arrived in the village, St Francis began to visit with the people. First he stopped in on the butcher. Next a visit with the cobbler. Then a short walk to the home of a woman who'd recently buried her husband. After that a stop at the school to chat with the teacher. This continued throughout the morning. After some time, Francis told his disciple that it was time to return to the abbey. The student didn't understand. "But we came to preach," he reminded. "We haven't preached a sermon." "Haven't we?" questioned the elder. "People have watched us, listened to us, responded to us. Every word we have spoken, every deed we have done has been a sermon. We have preached all morning."

Have mercy on those that doubt. Save some by snatching them from the fire. Fearing God, have mercy on some, hating even the clothing contaminated by their sinful urges.

It's not that works save the Christian, but that works mark the Christian. So, what work is marking you? What effort are you putting forth, not to be saved by or noticed by someone, but what effort are you putting forth to show your faith? If you take life too serious, maybe you need some playtime in the Nursery or Children's Church. If you think life is a game, maybe you need to park a car, greet at the door or serve in the kitchen. If you think that there isn't anything you can do or you aren't needed, then you my friend, are believing a lie. Don't sit on your seat and wait for God to move your mountain. Pick up your shovel and get to work moving it, then God will give you the strength and the wisdom to move it. Become something in the Kingdom besides a chair warmer. It's always more fun to play in the game than to sit on the sidelines.

Remember, your temptations come from your desires. So be careful what you desire. Sometimes it isn't exactly what you wanted in the first place. But put the love of God first in everything and then love those around you.

Endurance: The fact or power of enduring an unpleasant or difficult process or situation without giving way

> **What defines a true believer of Jesus Christ? It isn't how a life begins or how it is lived but what condition the heart is in when it dies.**

He's dead! He's dead! My heart is shattered. I don't know what will I do now. I was with Him every day and just a few days ago He was speaking at church. How will I ever be able to go this week, knowing He won't be there, seeing the place He sat empty or filled with another person? My life seems so empty and worthless now. We had such great plans of sharing Gods love, He would preach the gospel and I would follow Him. Helping Him. I decided my job was to take care of Him. You know, fix His meals, wash His clothes, make sure He has had plenty of rest. But while I was sleeping, something terrible happened. It's all such a blur now. His last words to me still ring in my ears..... How precious those words are to me. He told me to be strong, He told me to remember Him. He told me not to quit or ever give up. But how can I do this without Him. I am still in shock. This was not what I had imagined our life would be. Jesus, why did you have to die?

Picturing myself going to the tomb heartbroken. I watched him die. I saw his body in the casket. Now going to spend some time at the gravesite... remembering. On the way thinking about every last holiday, every last birthday, every last moment spent with him. Then upon arrival I find his grave had been messed with. The flowers were set to the side, the dirt removed. What happened? How could they. Then to see his body gone? Devastation above all. How could they do this. Don't they know I love him. Don't they know He was my world. Then to see someone standing not too far away. I blamed them, what did you do? Who took him? Where is he? Questions riveting my mind. Only to hear that familiar voice say my name. He didn't say anyone else's name. He said mine. At that moment I recognize Him. Tears of relief sweep over me. My hope is alive.

Experiencing the death of someone so close to me, I can only imagine the joy. Praise The Lord. Oh death where is your sting? There is victory over death, hell and the grave!!!! Bring it now Lord! Bring it now!

I went to the place they buried him. He's not there
He is ALIVE!! My Jesus is Alive.

I went outside this morning and saw the rose bush that someone gave me in memory of my mom. The other day it was a bunch of dead sticks with thorns. This morning I went out a there it had new green leaves all over it. Except it wasn't very pretty. There were still a lot of dead thorny stems left all over it from last year's flowers. Last year it was covered with beautiful sweet smelling roses. So I got my pruning shears and began the process of removing the dead stems. Made me think about my life right now, today. I have lots of "dead stems" in my life. Last year they may have been nice, but this year they are dead. New life is trying to emerge but the dead life is hindering it. Know what I mean? So the pruning begins. Pruning hurts, it's uncomfortable, but without it I would have a life with a bunch of dead thorny places with a just a few leaves trying to survive. Most of the time we know what the dead places are in our lives, and we know they need removed. But we want to hang on to them. I'm in the midst of being pruned, I don't like it much, but it is my hope that once it's finished I will be a beautiful rose bush full of amazing roses.

Is your money short? Are you working harder? Making more money yet it doesn't meet your needs? Can a man rob God? Absolutely. How? In tithes and offerings. When we don't give our tithe and we don't give any offerings we are asking God not to bless our blessings. Yep, it's true. God will either bless your blessings or curse them. I just read this in Malachi, read it yourself. It's in your hands. It's completely up to you. You determine whether your blessings are blessed or whether your blessings aren't. Having a job is a blessing, but it's not good enough. Having a good family is a blessing, but they are sick, lost and filled with turmoil. Having a home is a blessing, but it's falling apart around you. Now, are your blessings blessed or not. The little you have isn't enough. It seems that it never is. God wants to bless you, but...... If you aren't doing your part, He won't do His.

God, you and I have a problem. I just read that I can't love you and money. So one of you will have to go. I can hold money in my hand and I can't see or even touch you. I can work hard and make more money but I can't work my way into heaven. I read that too. So I just wanted to let you know I am weighing out my options. I have been watching people in general. Those that don't claim to know you seem pretty happy. I've been watching church people. God have you noticed how miserable some of them act. In fact they don't act much different than those that don't go at all. I've known some who were addicted to terrible things, turn into some really good guys. But some of the others that say they follow you, well, I'd rather hang out with someone else. So God, if you aren't too busy today, I'm making a list of the good things about money and you. So far my money list is much longer. If you want you can jump in any time and help me write your list.

Isn't that what we do? Weigh God out with money and material things? And some or most of the time God loses. We trade what we can't touch for things we can touch. We compare one person to the next and choose God or not, based on them. Good grief, what are we doing? That isn't how God works at all. In fact I am thrilled God doesn't do that.

So I imagine God has a list. He compares me to His disciples like Peter, James, John then He compares me to Paul, Silas, Philip and Timothy. Then He compares me to those who have died for the gospel in countries all over the world. Then He compares me to great teachers, preachers. Good grief! I wouldn't even begin to compare to any of them. Not because I am a woman, but because I don't live my life like they did. God doesn't compare me like that. He doesn't put me and money in the same category and then choose. He chose me a long time ago. I chose Him a few years ago. I'm glad God doesn't compare me to things the way I compare Him to things. I would lose every time. God loves me. (Period) That is all I NEED to know. Everything else His word tells me, is just icing on the cake.

Race towards the goal that is set before you. The prize is Heavenly.

Ok, you messed up. Do you think I'm looking for someone perfect? I mean really. Is that what you think? Do you really think you could ever be perfect in my eyes? Maybe if there had never been a law, then maybe, just maybe. The law reveals your imperfections, your failures. Surely without it you would be perfect in my eyes. Wait, no I remember before the law I destroyed the world. With a flood like you could never even imagine and then only one man and his immediate family was saved. So, do you get it yet? I'm not looking for perfection. My Son took care of that part. I'm looking for the "willing". Yep, that's it. The "willing". Are you "willing" to be called mine? Are you "willing" to put down your plans and dreams to follow me? Those who aren't willing, will go no further than just trying to obey the law. They will continue to wallow in their imperfections and their failures. But you, yes you!

I don't care what you've done, where you have been, what you have promised, what you said or been called... Are you "willing". If you are willing then so am I.

My husband asked the other night a question. "What good thing has God done for you today?" A few answered the normal Christian answers. So here is mine. I tend to fail and lose my temper at the ones I love the most. Then I let satan depress me and make me feel so inadequate to do anything for God. But my God is so awesome He lets me read, in His word, about people just like me. They started off not knowing Him, then they became His friend. They messed up made stupid decisions. They paid a price for their acts. But God still loved them, still used them and blessed them. Not because they messed up, but because He loved them. What wonderful thing has God done for you this week? Be specific. There are those who may read it and be encouraged.

Be careful what you do and say. There is always someone watching.

I didn't want my life to get this way. Somewhere it took a wrong path. I've hurt my mom. I've hurt my dad and I've embarrassed my family and myself. I am despised by the church. I hate myself so much. I have been kicked out of my home and now I live in the most detestable place, among the dead. I've got so many scars, so many bruises, so many gashes and cuts, I look horrible. I've gotten myself into this position and I don't know how to get out. It is as if an evil thing has taken over my life, my body, my mind and my soul. Suddenly I begin screaming obscenities as loud as I can.....

Everyone is in the boat heading across the sea. I am in the boat with Him. He spoke with such authority, I was compelled to follow Him. All I know is we are going to the other side. I don't know why. The crowd is following in other boats. Such wise words, such passion, such knowledge. As I watch Him, He lays down in the boat and has fallen asleep. Who is this man. Suddenly a storm. Waves begin crashing over the sides of the boat. We are scooping out as much water as we can to keep it afloat, but it just comes in faster and faster. The waves are tossing all the boats around like toys and He is still sleeping. How? One of His own wakes Him, stretching and apparently in no hurry, He stands up and says, "Hush, be quiet, be still." Did you see that? Even the sea and the wind obeyed Him. Who is this man, I mean really? We know He has more wisdom than we have ever seen, more knowledge, yet is humble and kind. Now even the wind and the sea obey Him.

Arriving on the other side, a crazed man approaches us. Yelling apparently at Him. "Why are you here? Just to torment us?" The closer this man gets I notice he is naked, filthy and disgusting. Then I notice where it looks like he is living, in a cemetery next to the sea. Who would live there? Doesn't He know, if anyone touches him they become unclean? Yet closer and closer He gets. I now notice the smell. He smells like death. The closer He gets to Him the more I can see that he is unable to stand. The nasty man doesn't stop screaming at Him. But his screaming seems to be turning into begging now. Suddenly the air goes quiet. Then He bends down and picks the naked man up. He touched him. Why would He touch him? "Get him some clothes", He says, "get him some food and water as well". A gentleness and kindness like I have never seen. It happened right in front of me. Grace and mercy wrapped with love. This man I heard speaking God's word with such passion. This man that just spoke to the wind and the waves. This man who spoke to pure evil...... who is He?

A snake will investigate every inch of its cage checking for a way to escape. It will go along the bottom. It will crawl up each side and each corner. It will bump every inch of the top, searching and looking for a way out. No matter how small the tiny gap is, it will become its way out. This is my thought this morning... Satan is exactly the same way, he is looking for a way not out of your life, but into your life. He goes around tapping and bumping every square inch of your life until he finds the smallest gap.

As long as we have human flesh, he finds a way in. It doesn't matter how spiritual we think we are. How holy or blameless. The tiniest, weakest area is exactly what he is looking for. He doesn't wait to be invited. It is a constant bump, tap, bump, tap until he gets in. He will make us weary, tired, depressed, angry, or he may even let us be happy, wealthy, and be full of energy. But it's the constant tap, the incessant bump just to get in. Once he is in, he infects quickly. He doesn't give up. My defeat doesn't happen at the tapping or the bumping. My defeat doesn't happen upon the entering. It happens during the lingering. Jesus says to immediately remove him. To stay on guard against him. To not give him one moment or thought. Yet, I find myself justifying why I am angry at someone or something (bump, tap). If I have to justify it, then it is probably wrong. (Right?).

He (Satan) goes around seeking anywhere he can sneak in, barge in, take over and destroy. The best defense is a awesome offense. The Holy Spirit is seeking as well. Only He goes around looking for someone to be strong in. Someone He can work through and work with. That someone could be you. Make sure today you let the right one in and keep the wrong one out. And even if you fail, go ahead and let the right one in. He can easily defeat the wrong one.

Sometimes I want to take a break from life, so...... I take a nap.

My morning reading has my thoughts going. He called for everyone, not just his closest friends, to come to him. He had something important to tell all of them (believers and unbelievers). "If you desire to follow me, then you must deny yourself. (Deny what? Your other desires, your other wants, your dreams, etc) Then you will take up your cross (not a comfortable thing to carry. It doesn't leave room for pride and selfishness. The cross is awkward and heavy. It isn't easy to carry. It smells of death) and then you can follow me (a new life). For if you desire to save your life (the life that has lead you down the wrong road. The life that keeps taking and taking. The life that the world believes is right), you will lose it. But if you are willing to lose your life (Not just because things aren't going your way. Not to hide or make someone think your holy. Not to get out of your responsibilities) but because of me and my words that I have taught you. The words that bring life to your soul. Then you will save your true life, your eternal life. Because what profit is it if you get everything you want in life and lose the only eternal thing you have, your soul? What is a soul worth? What is your soul worth? Jesus thought it was worth everything.

There are seasons in life when we feel so overwhelmed with the way things are going. Too many bills and not enough money. Vehicle issues, house issues, family troubles, sicknesses, etc. Everyone is put through the fire, so you aren't alone, God isn't picking on you. This is what I am seeing and slowly learning. I have been where I am before. I have fought the same battles and I made it. So the battles you are going through right now, are not eternal. You have fought them before. Remember? God didn't leave you then and He isn't going to leave you now. Even gold is purified by going through the fire over and over again. The waste is removed, and it is put through it again. It isn't fun, but once you've gone through it and look back, you can see every step you took. The right ones and the wrong ones. Remember the right ones, you may need to follow those again. We have a very good God and a very terrible adversary.

This morning I took my daughters puppy out to potty. She is a tiny, little eight week old Yorkie. I sat her on the shortest grass and then walked a few feet away to the porch to watch her. We have a set of stairs that are on the south side of the porch that she can climb to get back on the porch. But this morning she tried to climb the 1 big stair (for her) that is on the east side of the porch. She was barely able to get her front feet on the big stair, so she whined. She would walk a few inches below the same stair and try to climb the stair again. I let her do that for a few minutes, while she whined. She could see me and she wanted to be at my feet. All the while I knew about the south side stairs. They are the stairs that she usually uses (the short ones). So I chose not to pick her up, but to show her the right stairs. So I stepped down and had her follow me. Someday, she will be big enough to climb the bigger stair. But right now, she needs to use the smaller stairs.

It got me to thinking..... Right now I need to use the smaller stairs to get where I need to go. I can see Him in the different areas of my life, but sometimes I try to use ways that aren't right for me. They are the stairs that today (and maybe today is the last day) that I am not ready to use. He doesn't scold me, but I whine anyway because I see others using the bigger stairs. I can't let envy get the better of me, because I'm still stuck on using the smaller stairs. He knows me, better than I know myself. He understands my limits and my dreams. There are days that He pushes me gently to do things that aren't in my comfort zone. And there are days that I keep trying to do things that are not meant for me to do. So He gets down to where I am, among my discouragements, my failures, my broken heart and gives me hope so I can follow Him to the right place. He isn't a God that will let you stay where you are. He is a God that will come where you are and lead you out. He wants to show you the right way and at the right time. He will show you an even better way. So be patient while you are climbing your stairs. Someday your steps will get bigger.

Don't wait until later to say or do something for someone. Later doesn't always come back around.

I went outside this morning. What a beautiful morning. The quiet sounds of life chirping from the trees. The gentle breeze, the calmness of a sunrise. As I stood there the busyness of life began to creep in. The call of a distant black bird was replaced by the sound of a truck driving by. When God speaks sometimes it is a whisper. Sometimes it's a shout. But either way He still speaks. The signs of life are sometimes replaced by the busyness of life. One brings wonder and one brings chaos. Don't forget that both are life. I wish I could sit on my porch and just enjoy the quiet sounds of nature, but that isn't how life is. Life is a lot of ups and downs. A lot like a heart beat or a breath. Life can't be all up and it won't be all down. Life can't always be inhaled, and you can't exhale only. It takes both the ups and downs. Breathing in and out. Life ends with a flat line and the absence of breath. Don't let the busyness of life drown out the signs of life. Stop and enjoy what God is doing. He created you to be more than you could ever imagine. Even if you were created for one moment in time, for one task. You never know what that one moment may create. You never know what that one task might start. It only takes a spark to start a fire.

Love that the sun is shining outside. May the Son shine on your heart today and chase away every evil and dark place if you go looking for dark places, you will find them. If you are looking for the Light, you will find it as well.

It is going to be a beautiful day!! Remember saying... Where is spring? Here it is! The apple tree blossoms and each day more blossoms grow. Each day it gets more beautiful. But now... The blossoms are blowing away in the wind. Why? So the fruit can grow.

Men, it is time to be men. Women, it is time to let men lead. It is time for a revival in our men. Women you won't be left out. But stand aside.... We need men who will put their shoulder to the plow and work hard for the Gospel of Jesus Christ. Praying with a sword in their hand, a passion in their heart, a drive in their soul...... for the lost. The lost are just that, lost. If you don't go looking for them, they won't be found. They need the truth, and the truth is..... Jesus loves them. He wants to better their life by being a part of their life.

Young women.... it is time to raise your standards. Not to lower them. So what you may be "alone"..... How else do you expect to get a man that will be all you need, (not want) him to be? By lowering your standards, by giving in to the idea that you will never find a guy. Come on and get real. If you raise your standards and don't give in, the men will have to raise theirs. A good man isn't determined by his position in life, but by his love first for God and second for his family.

Older men! Older women!..... it's time. Stop saying "been there, done that" and complaining about how things are going. That things just aren't how it used to be. How it used to be may have work then, but may not work now. Start leading, stop complaining. Do our young people see a difference in you? Do they see someone who has been on their knees? Do they hear in your voice strength and hope or do they hear defeat? Do they see passion or do they see us just getting by? Do they see us fighting or do they see us giving in? We try not to stir up trouble, and allow sin to walk right into our lives. Stop it, repent and get up and do something! Pray for leading. Pray for guidance and then do it. Your age doesn't matter, but your heart does.

No matter what happens today, I know who will holds my hand and will never let go. It's amazing how much stronger I feel, knowing the creator of all things seen and unseen loves me.

Awesome day. Heard my favorite preacher this morning. I love it when God inspires him to say the things he does. The world is looking at the church and saying "Jesus, are you in there?" (Off of the idea of lost boys trying to decide if Peter Pan is truly Peter Pan grown up. The young lost boy pulls back and stretches the skin of Peters face until he see something that resembles him.) that statement "Jesus are you in there?" Really struck a chord with me. Does the world see Jesus in me, in my life? Because there are days when I have forgotten who I am and who the church is supposed to be. That the wrinkles and time has erased my resemblance of Him. May the world not stop looking for Jesus and may the lost boys find the resemblance once again.

When my husband and I finished mowing and weed eating this weekend, I looked at how beautiful the yard looks. I took a little pride in knowing.... we got it all done and it looks good. At that moment I didn't begin scheduling the next mow. I just enjoyed what we had accomplished. Have you ever mowed a yard so good, so perfect that you never had to mow it again? Nope. Life is like that..... it just keeps growing. Sometimes the weeds get a little overwhelming don't they? So what do we do? Well, we start with the mower blades up high and mow it. Then we lower the blades and mow it again and then again, until it's right. We have to do life the same way. I t gets overwhelming at times. Things just keep happening. Bang, Bang, Bang.... Weeds get higher. Life gets tougher. So what do you do? Give up? Nope, you raise the blades and get to work..... Do what you can today, nothing more, nothing less. Then tomorrow.... do it all over again. Don't quit, don't give up. Pray for guidance. Read His word for knowledge. Ask for understanding and then rest in knowing God has used hard places in life to speak loudly to those who are listening.

I don't trust God because He has answered every prayer.
I don't love Him because He gives me material things.

> **I don't even believe in Him because that's how I was
> raised. Just trust Him. Just love Him. Just believe Him.**

Sweet smelling surprises... Sometimes life just stinks. But then, sometimes even for just a moment, a sweet smell shows up. Sitting outside drinking my morning coffee, I remembered some trash that I had seen yesterday on the driveway. So I decided to go pick it up. My driveway is a little long and has ditches on each side with lots of weeds. These weeds seem to collect trash that gets blown around. With my coffee in hand I begin my walk. I pick up the trash and I pass the sweetest smelling honeysuckle bush. Oh my! I stopped just to enjoy that smell. To some these are annoying vines. To me, they are full of memories with my dad. We would go for a walks and he would tell me about the trees. He would break off a leaf and rub it in his hands to smell it. He would tell me the name of the tree and have me to smell the crumpled leaf. Then we would continue our walk. But when we would pass a wild honeysuckle bush, he would always stop and close his eyes and smell the aroma that would fill the air around it. I catch myself doing that more often. Just stopping for a moment to see a sunrise, to enjoy the sound of a child's laugh, to be encouraged by the affection of an older couple holding hands. To take the time to kiss my husband, hug my children. pet on my dogs. I get too busy with life and forget to stop and enjoy it.

My dad is still teaching me that today. Because of him, I drive a little slower, walk a little slower, look around a lot more and it drives my family crazy. Why? Life is passing too quickly. I feel like I have missed so much of it by hurrying everywhere. I'm learning to stop, rub some leafs together and smell the honeysuckles. To keep my eyes open to the God given wonders, God made miracles around me. There is always a lesson in there somewhere.

The last picture of this rose bush wasn't so pretty. I had just cut all the old dead flowers off. Now look, there are even more flowers now than there was before. When life is filled with troubles and you aren't sure you can go on. Hang on to Jesus and believe. He may just be preparing you for greater things.

He appears to some as God almighty, but they do not know Him as Lord. But He knows your name and wants to make himself known to you. He speaks through His word, His creation. He speaks through gentle rains and loud claps of thunder. But you aren't listening. Your spirit is in such anguish because of the things that have put you in bondage. He is still God and He is still able to deliver you. It may get worse before it gets better. Don't give up. Keep the faith. It took 40 years to take a 3 day journey. So be strong and courageous and don't be afraid because of them. For your God goes with you and He will protect you and guide you. He will be the fire at night and the cloud in the day. He will lead you through this present wilderness and set your feet on His promises. Don't worry about tomorrow. There are enough concerns for today. One step, one day at a time. Remember He loves you.

They didn't realize their power, but the enemy did. So he (the enemy) did his best to break them. He made them work hard. He beat them, threatened them and put them in bondage. The enemy did all that he could do to destroy their hope, their faith and therefore he destroyed their power. They were trying to live on yesterday's blessings, last year's hopes and their father's dreams. They lost sight of tomorrow's promises. They had forgotten that this was not home. So they put up with the abuse. They bowed to the enemy. They gave in to fear and defeat, never knowing that the enemy was afraid of them.

We are children of God. Not just any God, but a holy and just God. We are children of the creator of all things. We have been chosen for more than we will allow ourselves to believe. Revive yourself once again and remember who you are in Christ. Then take your stand against the enemy. He already knows you have more power than him. He just doesn't want you to come to the knowledge of, or remember, it and then use it against him. My weapons are not of this flesh, but they are mighty in the power of God.

Hey it's Friday!! I have a friend and He is awesome. He isn't like any of my other friends. No matter what, I know He always has my best interest at hand. When I need someone to talk to, He is there. When I need someone to put me back in my place, He is good at that too. He has heard me yell, cry, give up and then when I'm all done, He picks me up and lets me know He still loves me and believes in me. I can call Him anytime, anywhere. I don't think He even sleeps. My husband loves that He and I are so close. In fact it helps our marriage out a lot. You see, He is my husband's best friend too. My husband knows we don't have that worldly kind of relationship, it is so much more than that. My friend always has the right words to say. Sometimes I don't like it, but I need to hear it. I would love to introduce my friend to you. His name is Jesus.

That's it, I have had enough. I can't take another moment of it. I'm coming out!! I am 100% female! For almost 48 years I have never wanted to be anything else. I am happily married to a man for almost 23 years. Man and woman. I am a follower of Jesus Christ for almost 24 years. I believe in equal rights but not special rights. I believe what the Bible says about sin, forgiveness, salvation, Heaven and Hell. There is only One True God, One

Savior and One Holy Spirit. There is only one true Word of God. I don't believe all religions are true. I don't believe just because you think you are good you go to Heaven. I believe there is still good in this world and there will be until the day Jesus comes back. Don't give me excuses on why you can't be a decent Christian. Don't talk to me about drunkenness being ok. That sex before marriage is alright. That living a life of sin is over looked by a Holy God. That God will compromise to justify your sin. I won't say I'm sorry if I stepped on your toes. I would rather be applauded by God than by man. When Jesus comes back you can have everything I leave behind. I won't need them anymore anyway. I'm only going to take the eternal things with me. There I feel better. No more hiding.

The word of God is being preached everyday by His creation. Whether it's a small puppy trying to climb the stairs or a bird searching for food and safety. A rose bush growing or planting and maintaining a garden. Each day I witness God's word coming to life in the things around me. I only have to be still for a moment to notice them. God's word wasn't written to be scarcely understood. But it was written simply to point our "soul" focus towards Him. Ask Him today to show you something about himself. Then open your eyes and your heart and be still for a moment. He will answer you. His creation confirms it.

Been reading Old Testament lately. We aren't too different from the Israelites. After seeing God do amazing things, we forget and complain. "It's too hot. I'm too tired. Life's too hard." Wa wa wa God got tired of hearing them cry many times and wanted to end them. But one man stood up for them. Moses. Jesus is the one who stands up for us now. No matter how much we whine and complain, his love never changes. Ever wonder if our whining hinders our prayers? If our complaining extends our time in the hard places? Pray and keep praying. Believe and keep believing. Ask and keep asking. Complaining never solved anything. Overcoming does.

It isn't the water that saves you, it's the prayer. It isn't the words, it's the broken heart. There isn't a special formula, a program, a book or a special person on this earth that can save you. It's the love of a Holy God, a sacrificing Savior, it's the presence of a the Holy Spirit. This doesn't promise a perfect life, but it does promise a forgiven one. I can't be perfect, but I can be forgiven.

On my mind this morning is this..... Offense or Defense. Every game has offensive plays and defensive plays. Few players are good at both. Why? Maybe because those who are on the defensive side are worried too much about not letting the other score. They play not to lose. Maybe those who are on the offensive side are concerned too much about keeping score, usually their own, at the cost of the team and the victory. I've never played sports. My daughters are more than willing and constantly reminding me of this. But I watch the game. This I know..... every player has a weakness. Once their weakness is revealed they are vulnerable. If you walk around defeated, you won't be able to score. So, stop keeping your score and definitely stop keeping the score of others. You aren't ignorant of the ways of Satan. Stop acting like it. Start being a team player.

I looked up the characteristics of a TEAM player. Now let's see if you are one.

1. Demonstrates reliability. Ouch!
2. Communicates constructively. Uh oh,
3. Listens actively. are you listening?
4. Is an active participant... hmmm.

5. Shares openly and willingly. (no secrets)
6. Cooperates and pitches in to help. (it isn't all about you)
7. Commitment to the team. (teams biggest fan or critic?)
8. A problem solver, (not problem maker).
9. Demonstrates flexibility. (if it doesn't go your way, don't cry about it).
10. Treats others in a respectful and supportive manner. (Even if you don't like what they are doing.)

I'll admit it, according to this I am not a good team player, so I will start working on this today. Our Heavenly Father has already told us who wins and who loses. God is good. He's got this, now get with it. Increase your offense, increase your defense and get in the game. Stop playing only defense, and jump in on the offense. Stop playing only offense and jump in on the defense. The team needs you.

God will go to great lengths to get you where you should be. What man can mean for evil, God can use for good.

Smile.... lift up and encourage those around you. Laugh at yourself when things don't go right.

Many people I know are in desperate situations. Some are very vocal about their needs and situations. Some are very quiet about them. Some grumble and complain. Some pray and believe. God hears them all. He hears the grumbles and He hears the cries for help. He listens to their prayers. Remember the answered prayers of the past, but at the same time don't expect that one prayer to be the last one you will ever need to pray. Whether it is a need or forgiveness, healing or deliverance. Keep praying. I've never seen a trash can empty for long. It seems to fill up on a regular basis. Nor have I ever seen a garden that never needed tending. Prayer regular and grumble less often. Both can change you, but only one can improve your situation.

My God requires a daily sacrifice..... me. Every day I fail Him in some way. With my attitude or things I say and do. For the most part I reflect very little of who my Jesus really is and what He looks like. Right now all I see is a blurry image when I look in the mirror. I am so glad it isn't so with Him. He sees me clearly and loves me. He loves me so much, He doesn't want to leave me in the same condition He found me in. So sometimes subtle and sometimes not so subtle, changes are made within my heart, my soul and my mind. A change of heart, a change of attitude, changes in the way I see things and understand the things of God. I am not a philosopher. I don't study Greek. I can't read or understand Hebrew. I am not a bible scholar. But I am his child and I know He is proud of me. Not because I am perfect, but just because I am His. He understands me and knows who I am. You may not realize right now who you are in Him, but I promise, if you let Him, He will change your life. He hasn't made me richer, in the worlds eyes, but I have treasures set before me in heaven that no man can touch or take away.

Go check it out. That land over there. It is the land we are going to inherit. Then come back and tell us all what you have seen. Bring back some of the fruits and vegetables. Take pictures, remember everything you can, and share it all with us.

Twelve leave for the great adventure..... Twelve come back and report... "The land is amazing. Here is the fruit and here are the vegetables". They show the pictures of the grazing fields, the lakes and the creeks. "It's beautiful", all twelve report. But ten of them say, "there are people there and they are big and strong and we have heard how horrible they are. We can't move in there while they are there." Only two would say we can do it. Only two would say "it's ours! Let's go get it". Only two were willing to move in. Did God lie? Didn't He promise it was theirs? Didn't He say just cross over and take it? But the majority ruled. They didn't go. So they wandered for forty years in the deserted and unfruitful places. They didn't want to have to do "anything" to get the land God promised them.

Are we like them? Do we think that the problems are too big? The intended circumstances too hard? Is life too short to go after the promises of God? Did it take much to convince you to back off from doing what God intended for you to do? What was it? Your reputation, money, time, being made fun of? Did someone just say "you can't do it?"? Was your life threatened? Were you going to have to give up too much? What was it that stopped you? If your promise is just out of reach and you needed to let go of that one thing to grab it, would you? If your promise was just across the river, would you cross it? If Heaven were so close that you could see it, so close that you could touch it, so close you could hear the angels singing... what would stop you from grabbing it?

We fall short a lot. Leaving our promises just out of reach because we wouldn't let go of something to grab it. They are your promises and they are right there. Sometimes so close we can smell them. So close we can feel them. If we have to fight for it... might as well be a million miles away. God gave us promises. Let's don't let anything keep us from receiving them.

Ever been lost? The fear of being lost is over powering. The time between knowing where you are and being lost can be few minutes or a few miles. When you are lost all you need is directions. Being lost will cause you to go to places you have never been. When you are lost you begin to search for something familiar or somewhere safe. We don't set out to get lost, it just happens. The moment you receive the right directions, all fear leaves and all darkness is chased away because you know where you are. Your eyes that couldn't focus now focus. Your heart that was filled with fear becomes filled with hope.

I was reminded this morning about a time I was lost in St. Louis. It only took missing my turn. I had a GPS but I had the voice on silent. I tried just looking at it instead of listening to it. My destination was only 20 minutes away from where I was, but I was downtown, going every direction but the right one. The moment I knew I was lost, my heart began beating fast. I began to sweat and became anxious. All kinds of visions of disappearing and never being found entered my mind. I began repeating over and over again, "Jesus, help me". My husband called and asked me if I had made it yet. I told him that I was lost in St. Louis driving around downtown. I'm sure he could hear the fear and the panic in my voice. I told him I needed to get off the phone so I could pay attention to the traffic. I kept driving and the more I drove, the more lost and fearful I became.

Then I decided to stop and I pull into a parking lot. I leaned over to the GPS and searched for the sound. I turned it on and turned it up. The GPS knew right where I was and it knew where I wanted to go. Once I started listening to it, all my anxiousness left and I was confident again that I could get there. I followed the GPS voice closely. Every turn, every road, every stop until I reached my destination.

The lesson I learned... If you want to get where you are going, sometimes you have to turn your ears on and listen to someone who knows what roads to take to get you there. God knows where you are and He knows your destination. Trust Him, follow Him and I promise, He will get you there.

You can be lost anywhere and anytime. Sometimes it's spiritual. Life has caused you to lose your directions. Life has hidden the right path from your sight. Life has led you to a point of hopelessness. The path you chose hasn't led you to the places you wanted to go. For you, the only thing you need is Jesus. Always know He will lead you home.

You don't have to face today alone. Don't you know I will never leave you? Don't you understand that I will never forget you. It isn't My will that everything go your way. My will is that you follow Me. I created you to do great things. But you are settling for the lesser. I created you to speak my words, but you rarely say them. I created you to share and to bless others, but you have grown stingy and self centered. You don't have to face today alone because I still love you and I am still with you. So hold your head up and talk to me,. Give me all your fears, all your regrets and I will fill your emptiness with blessings. You don't have to face it alone, but it is your choice. I am just waiting for you to ask for my help, seek my face and knock on Heavens Gates.

It's one of those days that I just need to worship Him. To sit in His presence and feel Him. To trust in His strength and not mine. To rest in His peace. The battle isn't over, but it is time for refreshing and strengthening. Then I can get up and fight some more.

God is Faithful

When God says "No, don't do it." That is exactly what He means. No... don't do it. Consequences follow those who don't listen. Consequences will also follow those who do listen. If you listen and obey then good seeds will be planted and you will receive the wonderful fruits of them. If you do not listen and you do not obey, evil seeds are planted and you will receive the horrible fruits of them. It takes seeds time to germinate, to mature, to grow and then to harvest. We all want that instant gratification but the satisfaction and joy that follows is only short term. Working hard for something and then waiting patiently for it, lasts a lifetime.

No excuses will be accepted so just do it. Hit the share button concerning Jesus. Not just here on FB, but in your home, your community, your city, your nation and your world. Share Jesus. The best disciples got to know Him more by sharing Him. Not just reading about Him. Share what you know. Share what He has done for you and He will do more through you than you could ever imagine.

My day seems to start with the waking of my mind. Then it begins to control my thoughts and works its way around to my attitude. My attitude then seems to spill out onto those around me. You can choose today how you're attitude is going to affect those around you. When there is less of your wants and wills, there are more of His. Jesus loves me, this I know..... what better mind setter/ changer is there?

I agree with a young man that spoke last night. The church was designed to go out into the world and get them, not wait for them to come in. Thanks young man. You stuck your finger in my chest and said "do it". Not literally, we never even spoke. But your sermon both Sunday and Wednesday night was just what this ole lady needed.

The last thing Jesus told his disciples was what? To go! Go, not sit in a pew, not just pray about it, not just have meetings or develop programs, but to go. Go into all the world and preach the good news of Jesus Christ. We don't hear that much. Not out in the world, not the good news.

I loved this thought that he used. When I tell my children to clean their room before I get home, what do I, as a parent, expect when I get home? A clean room. Jesus told his disciples to go tell everyone the good news and make more disciples before he comes back. They did it and KEPT DOING IT (Jesus wasn't back yet.). That command has been passed down to us. The here and the now, you and me. If Jesus comes for you today, have you made any disciples? Have you accomplished the one task He told you to do? Or are you more interested in what's between your ears, who's between your elbows and who is sitting in your chair right now?

I'm talking to YOU. Are you more interested in inviting someone to church or inviting someone to meet Jesus? Are you more interested in inviting someone to the wedding, or asking someone to be the bride? I'm guilty. I ask more people to come to church than introducing them to the one who changed my life. Do I know more about the church than I do my Savior? Come on, let's get real. You are guilty too. And if church isn't going exactly the way YOU want it to go, you don't invite anyone to church.

So evidently, if you aren't inviting or introducing someone to Jesus, maybe you have the same problem with Him. Jesus isn't doing everything in your life exactly the way YOU want it and isn't doing it the exact way you want it done. Ouch, hit me too. Do we (you and I) really think, an excuse for not doing it will be good enough. Go ahead and think that, but it is not going to work. Try telling someone who died for it, that you prayed about it, read about it, had a meeting about it, talked with others about it, but never did it and call it trying. Try telling someone who gave their whole life telling people the good news, that you didn't know how, or what to say, yet you gossiped and shared bad things about other people. Go ahead.... They will accept that, won't they? I don't think so.

The longer you live in sin, the more you accept and justify it. But don't look down on each other because of it. Jesus didn't do that. He loved the unlovable and shared the love of God with them. He touched them without ever sinning, without ever becoming impure. He understood where they were. He reached out to them and loved them for who they were but didn't leave them that way. Be like Jesus.

Hope. What is it that brings you hope? Is it something that you can only touch? Is it something you can remember or is it something deeper? Our world, our nation, our communities and our own homes need reminded that there is hope.

So how do we get through days that seems to be harder than the last? We trust, believe and stand. Our God, our Father in Heaven, has said..... "Do not be afraid or be discouraged, For I am with you always." That tells me there will be times we may become afraid. That there will be days that we may become discouraged. But to not let those days or moments stay because Jesus is always right here with us, even until the end. Our reward will be worth it. Don't give up.

Look outside. See the trees? See how they sway in the wind? Can you see what is moving them? No. You can only see them moving but you know it is the wind. Can you tell from which direction the wind is blowing? No. You can only see what direction it is moving by the things it is blowing. God works like that. Sometimes you can't see Him, but you can feel Him and see what He is moving. Trust Him. He loves you. Always has and always will.

It is a daily surrender.... not a onetime surrender.

"Be strong and courageous! Do not be afraid or discouraged!" God said it to Abraham, his son Isaac, then his son Jacob. It was passed down to Joseph then on to Moses then spoken again to Joshua. It was spoken by Jesus to his disciples and it is still being said today to every man, woman, child and to every believer in Jesus Christ. It was not spoken because life was going to be easy. It was spoken because life was going to be hard. Who ever told you life was easy or that after you accept Jesus Christ, life is a piece of cake.... lied. God, creator of the universe, this world and everything in it did not speak these words to His enemy. He told the enemy to fear and be greatly afraid of Him. Yes, finances may be tighter than they have ever been, but don't stop giving. Sin may be invading every corner of your life, but you can stop sinning. Yes, this world seems to be getting worse and worse, but don't stop believing.

Choosing to walk with the Lord is the best thing I have ever done. It has never made me perfect, but it guides me to perfection. It hasn't given me the best of houses, fancy vacations or expensive jewelry. If that is what I am expecting or what I have been looking for, then I have been terribly mislead. I have a loving home. I take momentary vacations.... a walk to the pond, time with family at home each day. I have the precious jewelry that my loving children chose for me. I have the beautiful gifts my husband has given me over the last 22 years.

But the jewels I long to wear, I will never be able to afford on my own. Crowns of righteousness, stones of purity, jewels of redemption. The vacation I long for is out of this world. My vacation will be on streets of gold There will be walls of jasper. The music will be something my ears has never heard. It won't be dark or quiet, but filled with the loud sounds of angels and children of God singing praises to the One and only true God.

At Communion He said "Here is my body broken for you." What I heard was, "Here is my body broken for you, I knew your sins would crush you, so I took your punishment. I knew you would not be able to handle all of it. So I took it all". He said "here is my blood, poured out for you." What I heard... "Here is my blood poured out for you. My blood was my life and I gave you every drop so you could live. He said "it is finished." I heard. "I've done everything for you. All you have to do is accept this new life and love me". He said "I loved you before you ever even had a chance to get know me"...I didn't know what to say, so I cried.

Saying something simple..... Give me Jesus.
There is nothing on earth and no one else
that can give me what He can.

"So now: Fear GOD. Worship him in total commitment. Get rid of the gods your ancestors..... You, worship GOD. (Joshua 24:14 MSG)"If you decide that it's a bad thing to worship GOD, then choose a god you'd rather serve—and do it today. Choose one of the gods your ancestors worshiped, on whose land you're now living. As for me and my family, we'll worship GOD." (Joshua 24:15 MSG) The people answered, "We'd never forsake GOD! Never! We'd never leave GOD to worship other gods. (Joshua 24:16 MSG)

Well? You and I have made these same promises. I promise Lord if He will... Then I will... then I Fail. Then we complain because we think our God failed us, when we were the ones that failed Him. Our God loves us, and He is very jealous for our attention. There ARE consequences for serving other gods. Put God first in your life, love Him and serve Him. If not, then you will bow and serve another god.

Stop. Breathe and repeat after me. "God isn't finished with me yet. He loves me, right now, just as I am. And because He loves me, He won't leave me this way." (inhale, exhale slowly and repeat.) Feel better? Repeat as often as necessary today.

Ready for a new life? Feel like you have been buried alive? Feel dead inside? There is an answer.. Jesus.

Just in case you need reminded...... Jesus loves you. Your struggle, these circumstances and this season of life won't last forever. Each struggle can make you stronger, every circumstance can increase your wisdom and each season has a purpose. Just love Jesus back.

I listened to the world, and it told me how to live. How to treat people, how to take care of myself, how to do what I want, when I want. The world taught me how to love and be loved. I listened.... If I had paid attention I would have realized the world lies. Once I realized this, then true wisdom began. My life of sin was forgiven and I was made alive through Christ. As much as EVERYONE hates to be told what to do and when to do it and how to do it, we sure let the world, who hates God teach us how to live and to love. I still fail often, but His grace is greater than any of my failures.

Often it is hard to be positive in such a negative world. Remember, your smile can change the atmosphere of a room. Last night my bad attitude changed the atmosphere of my home. Where did it come from? A bad day? No. So where did it come from? Satan. All Satan wants to do is destroy our homes and relationships. He knows if he can do this he can make us weak. He can taint our integrity with our children, our family, our friends. Our integrity and attitude at home is as important, if not more important, as our integrity and attitude at work, at church or at the store.

So I have asked God to help me kill the giant that lives inside me. Just keeping my anger inside me quiet is no longer good enough. It still taints everything I do and say. So, how do you kill a giant? First, the giant must be exposed. That's the scary part.

Exposed? You mean seen? Yep. Giants can be destroyed. Giants can hide but when they do, it doesn't take much to bring them out. So they have to be exposed and then killed. Giants come in all shapes and sizes. Sometimes covered with justification and envy. Usually filled with pride and jealousy and dressed in anger and resentment.

But how do you kill one? David killed a giant with a rock and a sword. You and I have a rock and we have a sword, Jesus Christ and His word. Today, start killing those giants, no matter what their size. Stop letting them take over your attitude, your home, your job. If Jesus Christ really lives in you, then you were born to be a giant killer.

Sometimes our greatest battle is "Believing". Believe in the Lord Jesus Christ and you will be saved. Believe that with God all things are possible. Do we really know what it means? Have you thought about it. I looked it up and it means - to have confidence in the truth, the existence, or the reliability of something. Only if one believes in something can one act purposefully. Believe means to have confidence in the truth of something."

Don't you know, that our enemy is aware if he can shake your confidence, he can shake what you believe in. Throughout the Bible Jesus tells us to believe. We get so wrapped up in trying to attain knowledge, that sometimes we pass by "believing". We focus on the "Why's" instead of "Believing". The Pharisee's had tremendous amounts of knowledge. They understood prophecies, they quoted scriptures but..... they didn't believe. Everything they lived their life for was standing in front of them, Jesus. But they didn't believe. They fulfilled every prophecy concerning him and his death but they didn't believe. Do you believe? Don't answer too quickly, but answer truthfully. We are prisoners to lies, but truth sets us free.

Have confidence and believe in God's Word. Have boldness in believing everything in His Word is truth. Believe Jesus is Lord of all, King of all Kings. All that can be shaken will be shaken. Everything that can fall will fall. My confidence fell, but my faith stood it back up. My belief was shaken, but truth built it up stronger. I believe, but Jesus helped my unbelief. Believing + Faith = Unshakable.

God chooses some of the most simple things in life to speak to me. A Whisper....When God whispers my name, I want to be close enough to hear him. A Breeze...When He moves, I want to be close enough to feel his nudge. Sunlight.... Jesus chases my darkness away.

How could Jesus just walk into a place full of people that need him and nobody know he's there. For example the pool of Bethesda. Multitudes surrounded a pool they believed could heal them. Yet when the healer walks among them they didn't know or recognize him. Why? Were their eyes so fixed on the pool that they couldn't see when their source of healing was right there in their midst? Everyday Jesus walks among us. At work, at school, at the store, do we recognize him? Jesus wasn't one that went around trying to be the center of attention. He was the one who told them not to tell, but to go and sin no more.

Do you miss him when He is right next to you? Can you feel him when he's near or are your eyes like mine? Dull to seeing. Do you also have a heart hard from unbelieving?

Oh how I want to know when my Lord is close. How my soul longs to feel his presence. How my heart searches for his ever strengthening power. Yet my mind is so easily distracted. Forgive me Lord for allowing these temporary distractions to alter my focus away from you.

I believe Mary knew who her son was. She understood it from the moment the Angel spoke to her of his conception. I can only imagine how she sat back and watched as the Son of God grew from a small baby into a young man, full of great knowledge and wisdom and full of favor from God and man. I can only imagine as she followed him seeing the great miracles He performed, listening to the astounding way He could talk about his Father in Heaven, showing love to the lost and touching the untouchables. I can only imagine her waiting for the day everyone would see him for who He truly was, Jesus, the Son of the Living God. The Son of the Great "I Am", then they would love him. I can only imagine how she felt when He finally took his place as Savior. Yes, I believe Mary knew. What confidence she must have had, what courage, to know who her son was.

We need that confidence, to know who Jesus is in our lives. That He is bigger than any problem, bigger than any struggle, bigger than any fear. That the Great "I Am", is the living God. The God with no beginning and no end. The God that has all time is in His hands. Take confidence today in KNOWING who Jesus is and who you are to Him and in Him. Rest in His peace and at times hide in the shelter of His loving arms. Take confidence in KNOWING Jesus is coming back. This isn't all there is... there is more, so much more.

Today is Monday. I love Monday's. Why you say? Without a Monday there would not be a Sunday. God gave me seven days and I love all of them. Each day is a new beginning and new chance to start where you are and move forward with your life. Study your Bible and think about the words that were written and who wrote them. They were written for us to start our day new and fresh, walking in the wisdom of God. I could walk through this life without them, but I choose not to.

**A good song is made up of more than one note and each
note sounds different. If they all were the same notes,
would it not be redundant and boring? The body of Christ
is made up of many different parts. Each part doing
it's task well creates a body that works in harmony.**

Give the perfect gift this year..... Love. It's the one thing you
can take with you when you leave. It's the one thing that costs
everything, but even the poorest of the poor can afford it. Love...
the reason God sent his only Son. Love, the reason Jesus came.
Love, the reason Jesus died. You can't buy it at any retail store.
You won't find it on discount. You won't find it on any department
store shelf. There is no coupon to reduce its cost. If giving the gift
of Love was good enough for Jesus to come and die for me, then
it's good enough for me to give.

**Sometimes we feel like we are too broken too ever heal
But that is the thing my God is best at..... healing the broken.**

If God asked you to save the world what would you do?
Knowing that God had destroyed the world once and knowing
that everyone He had sent before was beaten, rejected and killed.
Would you be willing to try? What if God asked you to save your
nation? Would that be too much? What if He asked you to save
your community? Too much still? What if God asked you to save
the one standing next to you? That sounds easy enough, right?
That's just one person, right? Now what if you were standing next
to someone you didn't know or didn't like? Would that change
your answer? I mean it's just telling someone about Jesus, right?
How He changed your life, right? Maybe it's a stranger, maybe it's
a family member, maybe it's your friend, maybe...... But you said
yes didn't you.

It's Sunday and I know for some this is the only day they can sleep in. For some it's their only day off. For others the week has been so busy they just want to stay home. For others, it's a family day. For me it's a chance to be with my brother's and sister's in Christ Jesus, to worship the one who died for us. God is shaking the foundations of many. Don't worry, if your foundation isn't shaking, it will. As my life gets shaken, I want to be found faithful and strong. Not strong within myself but faithful and strong within the Lord. The church walls won't collapse. The ceiling won't cave in. Yep there are hypocrites there and yep there are talkers. Yep they are wrong. So come on, it's so much more fun to worship with friends than to be alone.

> *Sometimes you don't always know where the path goes, so you have to trust the one that built it. You can't always trust yourself to know the right way, but you can trust the one that created you.*

He is once again surrounded by people all begging him to do something for them. "Give me money, give me health, give me position, show me something amazing." Many were there for a show. To be entertained by the things He could do. Many times He had given them exactly what they asked for. Many times He had changed their life for the better, only for them to go back to where they were before, begging for the same things and not believing. It wasn't the begging that bothered him. It was the show they wanted him to perform and it was the lack of belief in their heart. He knew his gift wasn't for entertainment, but that is what many had tried to turn it in to.

So when a rich and well known man arrived begging for him to heal his son that was near death, He replied to the rich father, "All you want is a show, you don't really want to believe." But the father kept asking, "Will you come with me? My son is really sick and may already be dead. Will you come?" You see the father didn't even hear the first answer, he didn't want a show, he wanted a healing. So Jesus told him to go home, your son will live. So the rich and well known man left to go home. On his way home he met his servants and they told him his son was alive and the fever was gone. "What time did the fever leave?" he asked. When they told him what time it had left, he realized it was the exact time that Jesus had told him to go that his son would live. It was then that the rich father realized what had happened, then he and all his family became believers.

What would Jesus have to do for you? What sign, what wonder would cause you to believe? Would the answer you are searching for change your life for a lifetime or would you fall back, to where you were before? Do you need a sign or a miracle before you will believe or will you believe even if there is no answer, no miracle, no sign? "Blessed are those who have not seen me and still believe in me".

I haven't seen the dead raised. I haven't seen the lame walk, the blind see or the deaf hear, but I know Jesus can do it. I haven't seen money appear, or my bills get miraculously paid, but Jesus meets my every need. I have prayed prayers that He has answered, and I have prayed prayers that the answer hasn't come yet. But I believe, Jesus can. All I do is keep asking, keep believing, keep knocking until the answer comes.

What was it like being the last one? Everyone else was gone. Sitting alone with nothing left but memories. What was it like hearing someone teach and preach who had never met him, when you, were there when the water turned to wine, when the woman washed his feet with her tears, when the blind eyes were opened, when the lame walked, the demons were rebuked and then cross. It always leads to the cross. The memory of the cross... still ringing in your ears the words his best friend and leader spoke. "It is finished". The memories begin flooding your mind, from the day you met at the Sea of Galilee to the day his blood was running down that terrible cross. Just a touch of sadness, but then joy saturates your soul because you remember the tomb. Not just any tomb, but the once filled now empty tomb. Then your memory goes to the day you watched him with your own eyes rising up on the clouds into the heavens and the angel saying, He will be back.

John was still waiting for that day while he worked diligently telling everyone his story, the story of Christ. What was it like being the last disciple? The last one of twelve. I don't believe he was lonely. I believe he missed reminiscing with his fellow disciples, but not lonely.

I believe he was looking forward to seeing Jesus again. Though his eyes were dim with age he saw visions of heaven. Though his body was weak in strength, he had memories of his life here but his passions were for tomorrow. I am sure more than once he thought, today is the day of my salvation, today I will see my Lord.

It seems many of us want the passion for Christ, but few want the trials that lead to Him. Many want the glory, but few want the narrow walk. Stir up that passion, that longing to please Him, to love Him. Stir up those gifts inside you. Share your life changing story of how Jesus met and changed you. Many may not want to hear it, but there are those who are longing, waiting for someone to share. It won't just change their life, it will change yours.

Waiting for God to do some amazing things? In God's waiting room there are no chairs, because those who are waiting aren't sitting. They are moving, serving, asking, seeking and knocking.

My life has not been formed by perfect people. From the moment of my birth I have been surrounded by imperfect people. Divorces, unwed pregnancies, suicides, addicts, alcoholics, adulteries, hatred, racism, war and the list goes on. But... these are the people I love. They are family. I know that my God can use imperfect people to carry out his will. I know that my God can change hearts, attitudes, and circumstances. These people are now believers. Not just of Jesus Christ, but believers in Jesus Christ. I am proud to say every one of them is a big part of my family, not only in flesh but also in spirit.

God can and will use a willing vessel. He can forgive anything and anyone. No one is so far gone that they can't be forgiven and set free. The Bible proves it. Perfection can only be gained through the forgiveness of sins. That comes by believing in the sacrifice of His only Son Jesus Christ and by accepting him as the King and Lord of their life.

Now to be personal, it should have been me paying my debt. You see Jesus took my place. He has paid for my soul and I have accepted his gift even though I know I don't deserve it and know I can never repay him. I also know there is no gift that I could give that could ever match His. So I give Him my life. I fail often at following His commands. I mess up every day, but He is there ready to forgive. He is there loving me. For you see I have been redeemed. Jesus doesn't give up His redeemed. He paid too big of a price. He won't let His redeemed walk away easily. He calls out to them, whispering their name, loving them unconditionally.

You see It's your choice to walk away from Him. It has never been His choice for you to leave. He's still waiting for some of my family and friends to choose Him. So I will keep praying for them. Not because they deserve it, but because I love them and I know Jesus loves them too. Share His love today, this world is hurting and they need him.

Just believe. Happiness begins with believing you already have everything you need. Discontentment comes from wanting more than you need.

Everything she had was in her pocket. Going to church was all she had on her mind. Her clothes were not new. Her makeup was not flawless. Her shoes were not fashionable, but her heart was right. Her favorite time of the church service was about to happen. The weeks before she had nothing to give, but this week she did. Last week she came empty handed but this week she is giving all she has.

Here it comes. The offering plate. This time, as it passed her, she reached in her pocket and found every penny. Ten dollars and gave it all. She knew the joy of giving. She basked in the presence of God as she gave it all. Her heart was full of thankfulness. Her God was meeting every need. Just a few rows up sat a man that had plenty. He stood up and he reached into the front pocket of his new suit. There he found his leather wallet. He pushed around his money to find the right amount. There it is. He looked around to make sure people were watching as he placed a one hundred dollar bill in the plate. Smiling he sat down knowing he had placed the most in the offering that day. What would this poor church do without him? Probably have to close the doors. His heart was full of pride.

One gave out a need, the other out of abundance. One gave all, the other a small portion. One gave out of love and thanksgiving, the other out of pride. Who do you think received the biggest blessing? Oh how I love the Father and all the blessings He has given. I have never been able to out give Him.

Jesus has a name above all names. His name is higher than any President. His authority is greater than the U.N. Who should I fear? Nothing on this earth.

A manager was reported to his administrator about cheating the company. The administrator confronted the manager concerning it. The manager became very fearful. He had been doing his job for many years and it was all he knew. He didn't want to have to dig ditches. He didn't want to lose any of his belongings. So he thought about it and called the vendors that owed the company the most. He asked them how much they owed. The first vendor said one hundred thousand dollars. The manager changed that to seventy five thousand dollars. Then the manager called the second vendor and asked how much he owed. He said twenty five thousand dollars. The manager changed that to fifteen thousand dollars. Then the manager called another vendor and asked him how much he owed. He owed five thousand and the manager changed it to two thousand. When the administrator found out about the dealings of the manager and he commended him.

You see the manager wanted to make sure he had good favor with the vendors in hopes of getting employment there, or maybe the manager was correcting the mistakes he had made in hopes of keeping his current job. You see the manager was shrewd in his dealings. He did what he could to try to secure his future.

With fear driving the economy and the hearts of men, we are more willing to cheat and lie to get what we want. We are more willing to be dishonest. We are more willing to blame. Jesus told this story and then added, wouldn't it be great if the ones who believe in me did the same. That they went the extra mile to serve me. That they went beyond what was expected of them. That they loved me more than the things they search for. That they dealt with sin harshly instead of covering it up and ignoring it. No wonder many are depressed and moody. No wonder so many aren't happy and are full of bitterness. Our hearts weren't created to be filled with envy and strife. Our hearts were created to be filled with love and compassion.

Our enemy wants to destroy us. He wants to destroy you. Only by faith can we please God. Where is your faith? Make it a point to change your attitude. Make it a point to seek the favor of God rather than the favor of men. With God all things are possible.

The love of Christ does not compromise with sin. But defeats it through removing blame and bringing life back to that which once was dead. We were all born into sin and death. But through Christ we can be reborn into forgiveness and a new way of living. It all begins with turning your heart and life towards the Lord. It is the only thing that truly satisfies.

That last goodbye. For some it's a casket. For others it's a phone call, a text, or a letter. It could have been the car driving away. A plane leaving the airport or a train leaving the station. But this last goodbye wasn't anything like that. The days before were so strange. Fear, heartbreak, confusion followed by rejoicing, laughter and great expectation. This goodbye wasn't just an ending, it was a beginning. Would they have done things differently had they known? I don't think they would've.

"In or out?" That was the main question. They all agreed "In". Every moment for the last three years lead to that answer. Jesus prayed diligently for that answer in the garden. Jesus spoke clearly and gave them every reason to choose "out". Persecution, rejection and death. But Jesus also gave them the right reason to choose "In". Life everlasting with Him.

There was a peace and a joy that couldn't be moved out of their hearts that day. It lasted each one a lifetime. Their last goodbye wasn't when Jesus ascended. The last goodbye wasn't at the cross. The last goodbye was in a room filled with those who had been witnesses to the very same things. They said their final goodbyes to their old lives.

Peter, Andrew, James, John, Matthew, Thomas, Philip, Bartholomew, James, Simon, Judas(son of Simon) and the women who followed. They knew their decision meant death to everything they knew before. Their last goodbye wasn't the end, but a beginning to something greater.

Now you, my friend, have you said your last goodbye ? The good bye to your old life and walk the narrow path. Or are you choosing to live with your old life and walk the wider path? Don't make a quick decision. Think about it. Persecution, rejection, even death followed by life eternal with Jesus Christ ? Or just continue life as usual, followed by death and torment without Christ? It's your choice. Choose wisely. Count the cost and then decide.

The hands that can hold a universe and every star, are the same hands that can hold the ocean. Each and every drop. These are the same hands that placed all the stars in place. The same hands that can hold a single tear. He can mend a shattered heart,. He can revive a lifeless soul. He can breathe life into a motionless body. He can create anything out of nothing. He can crush a mountain or bury a sea.

He can, yes He can. He told the sky where to stay and gave the oceans its boundaries. He is bigger than any problem. He is greater than any trial. He is strength when we are weak and He will humble us when we get too proud. He can calm a sea and motivate an army. He is gentle, yet ruthless. He is God and yes He can. He can hold you, because He made you.

He can, oh yes He can. I wanted to remind you in case you forgot. Our God is able to help you no matter your problem. No matter how low or how high you go, He can reach you right where you are. There is no valley so low or mountain so high; There is no power on earth, no demon from hell; there is nothing, that's right, nothing, that can separate you from God.

Our amazing God.... In the beginning there was nothing. Then He spoke... for seven days He spoke everything into existence and on the seventh day the creator spoke rest into existence. Did God need to rest? Could God have been tired? No. God knew at the beginning of creation that his creation would need rest. So He instilled it to be.

When was the last time you rested and spent some time with Him? Spend some time with Him today. Rest in the fact that He's got this. The worries of this life are going to try to steal every word God ever spoke to you away. The worries of this world is going to try to kill every good thing in your life. Rest in the fact that God created everything, from the beginning. He's got this.

Remember His promises.... "I will be with you even unto the end of the world."

She is getting ready for a wedding. It was the wedding she had dreamed about. Flowers were ready. Going through the check list again and again. Everything seemed ready, everything seemed perfect. Now waiting for the day to arrive. She had been preparing for this day for months. Thoughts of being a perfect bride raced through her mind. Fears of not knowing how to do everything stirred her heart. Then the thought of him, the groom. The love they will share. Just the thought of the joy and happiness that would fill their home, chased away every fear she had.

It had been decided to do things differently in this wedding. The Father of the groom was to be in charge of the wedding. He chose the church and the reception hall. He had even chosen the bride for his son. Both the bride and the groom were waiting for the day to start. Neither knew the day or the hour. Neither had seen each other in a long time and the groom didn't know where the bride was staying.

At first they thought it was strange, but it added so much excitement. The Father told her to always be ready. At night leave a fire burning so the groom would see where she was. He told her that when the groom was close he would start playing his trumpet.

Then the wait came.. days.... weeks..... the excitement was fading..... months passed by.... where was the excitement now? At first she kept her makeup fresh. At first her hair was always done. At first everything was perfect. But now? Was the Father kidding? Was this wedding even going to happen or did he lie to her? The waiting was getting hard, and being ready was getting even harder. Her dress had lost its fullness. Her hair had fallen and her makeup was less than desirable. But she was still waiting.

In the middle of the night, she heard it. The trumpet. She jumped up and looked. The fire was out. "Oh no", she screamed, "someone light the fire"! There is no wood, they told her. With her messy dress, her fallen hair, her smeared makeup she ran outside to wait for him. The fire had stayed lit all this time, even during the day. But tonight of all nights it goes out. Surely, he had seen it at some time. Surely he knew where she was. So she stands outside in the cold. Waiting for her groom to come and get her and take her to the wedding of her dreams. She sends someone to get more wood while she waits. The trumpet sound was getting close. Her heart begins to race with excitement.

Then she looks at herself. How messy she was. Maybe he is far enough away that she can freshen up just a little. Running inside she quickly washes her face, fixes her hair, fluffs up her dress then runs outside. She begins to listen............ Where did it go? Where did he go? Oh no, she missed him. Anguish, despair, loss. Tears flow. She collapses. He's gone. She missed it. She wasn't ready

Jesus is the groom and we are his bride. The wedding is coming..... ready or not.

When the day seems so dark, remember you may be the only light some people will see. So keep your light pure and bright. Eyes are always drawn towards the light and someone may be using your light to walk through this life until they get a light of their own. Jesus is my light.

We are in a very dark room and you have the only flashlight. Some will be drawn to you because of your light. Others who like the darkness won't. In the darkness no one can see, everyone has the same problem. Some enjoy it, while others are afraid. What happens when you turn on the light? Darkness is chased away to the furthest corners of the room. Darkness can no longer roam free. This light was given to you to be shared with others. Shine your light for all to see. His word is a lamp for my feet and a light for my path.

> **The simplest way to stop doing wrong things,**
> **is to start saying NO.**

She's been sick for 12 years. She has spent all she has going to doctors. Her family all had to leave and her friends weren't allowed to be at her side. Her disease was too bad. Not a touch of a hand. Not a hug or a kiss for 12 years. Then she over hears the talk of a man. She hears of the blind man, a leper, a little girl. She hears of many sick people going to Him and leaving well. The thought begins to stir, "Maybe this is what I have been looking for. Maybe this is my cure." So she begins to wonder. Where is He? Where is He going?

Getting to him became an obsession. Nothing else mattered. But where is He. Then she overhears that He is close. Obsessed, she walks toward Him. She sees the crowd. It's huge. How will she ever get to him? Then the thoughts come. What will people say if they see me? I am not suppose to be around people. If they see me..... but if this is my hope....

She gets closer and closer, squeezing through the people, moving in closer and closer. She hears His voice. Oh what sweet words He was speaking. How comforting just to hear His voice. But his voice wasn't what she wanted. Pressing through and pushing on, the crowd just gets louder yelling His name. Everyone wants his attention. She gets as far as she can go, but it's not close enough. "On my knees" she says. "On my knees I will crawl the rest of the way." She gets just within reach and with everything she has she reaches out and touches just the edge of his clothing. Immediately she feels something different in her body. The pain is gone, the weakness... gone. Strength immediately begins to fill her. Then she hears his voice again. "Who touched me?" His followers said to him, "With so many people, how can you say who touched me." He said it again, "Who touched me?" She knew He meant her. Was He going to take it back? Was He mad that she, once filled with disease, touched Him? She stood and said "It was me, I touched you." He looked at her with such compassion, and then He gave her even more. She left that day with more than a healing. She left that day knowing she was forgiven. She was healed inside and out. She would remember his name for the rest of her life.... her Savior, Jesus.

Where are the lost? Where are those who need a reason to have hope? Open your eyes. They are sitting next to you at work, standing in line at the store, across the table from you. They could be your neighbor or your best friend. Take a chance.... and change a life. Funny, it may affect you more than you think.

Seems many want the blessings of God, without going thru the trials to get them. Blessings from God cannot be bought with money and gifts from God cannot be purchased. Seek the kingdom of God, put Him first and these things will be added to your life.

What inspires you? What motivates you? What causes you to want to do better, be better? Is it a movie? A song? A book? A person? We all need motivation. We need inspired to do something. Find your inspiration not just for today, but for life.

Run!........ Notice they are all running.... Notice some are in front, some are in the middle and some are behind. Their position didn't change the fact they love to run. Their different styles didn't keep them from running. They were running with a goal in mind... to finish.

What is your purpose? Are you a part of the problem or a part of the solution? The choice is yours. If you are the problem... stop it. If you want a solution, put your shoulder to the plow and join in and help. Are you sitting in the seat of scoffers? Don't you know the fields are ready for harvest, the workers are few and time is short. Don't complain, but join in and help.

Crying in her bed, praying things would change, wondering, will tomorrow be the same. Sitting outside at home alone staring at the stars, wondering why this life isn't how he dreamed it would be. She's all alone now and he's made a horrible mistake. Shattered dreams and broken promises line the hallways of their lives. She had lead a life of promiscuity. He had everything and more. All she wanted was love. All he wanted was her.

Hundreds of years apart and having never met, but their need was the same....they both needed a Savior. Mary searched for love, wanted commitment, but because of her past...... she couldn't find it. David was a king. He had everything he wanted, but her. Her husband was in the way. Because of the lust his heart, he committed murder and adultery. Mary found Jesus while she was laying in the dirt, in the filthiness of her life. David found the peace of God while he was standing in a palace mourning the death of their child. Lives of perfection? I don't think so. Lives in desperate need of a Savior? Absolutely. Only when we realize and become desperate for a Savior do we find him. While all along, He has been standing right there, ready to forgive and accept us.

The Face to Face Book

You see their lives aren't so different than ours today. We long for things to satisfy, to fill the void in our hearts. We want things that we shouldn't have and do our best to justify getting them. Only later to realize that Jesus was all we ever needed. If the void in your life is getting too big and the loneliness that it brings is overwhelming, please know your Savior is close to you. He is waiting for you to ask Him to not just remove that void, but fill it. That's why He came. He came to give you life and give you hope. Heaven is reachable but only through Jesus Christ.

Just travelers entering a city. Exhausted from days and days of traveling. The thought of a nice warm bed, a good hot shower and a sit down meal keep them moving. Upon their arrival they begin looking for a room to rent. From the cheapest room to the most expensive suite, all were booked. No friends or family to stay with. Another night in the car? Her back just couldn't take another night not being able to stretch out. Gone were the dreams of a shower or a sit down meal. But still hoping for a bed.... somewhere. The last motel just at the edge of town, check there they say. Upon arrival, "NO VACANCY" shined bright in the window. He goes in just to make sure. She followed just in case she could persuade the owner. "No room, I have no room". The owner, seeing the condition of the young woman, mentions his garage. "It's not clean, but it's warm. I keep a cot and blankets in there, if you want it, you can have it." The husband took the offer, he just couldn't ask his young wife to sleep in the car another night. Cuddled in the corner next to the old wood stove, the young couple talk for a few minutes and fall to sleep. The churning in her stomach woke her, she gently nudged her husband awake and said "it's time".

"Really" he said "are you sure?" "Yes, it's time" she said. Giving all he had just to get to this point, this wasn't his plan, this wasn't where he wanted it to happen and now it's time. He begins searching the garage for whatever he could find to make his wife

79

comfortable. He has never done this before. Should he leave and go get help or should he stay? Oh why did they leave everyone who could help, why? He told her he would be right back, he was getting the owner. Bolting through the garage door, running to the motel, banging on the door, the owner sleepily opened the door. "Can I help you?" he replied. "Yes, please come, it's my wife". Both running back to the garage, the young husband reaches his wife and says maybe he can help. When she finally looks into the eyes of the owner, she knew. It was him.

She recognized his eyes from her mother's photo. "Daddy" she says. The owner steps back and says "what did you call me?" "Daddy, it's you." They hadn't seen each other in over 20 years,. She was a baby when her mother left him. It was her desire to find her father once she was having a baby of her own.

Are you searching for something? If so, I know what it is. Our Heavenly Father put a longing desire for you to love him. He put it deep within the heart of every child. Even though children grow up and become adults, the need for a father is so deep that sometimes only hurts can hide it. Our Father in heaven loves you and wants you. His desire is to bless you and comfort you, to fill you and give you life. Seek Him today, put Him first in your life. He's been longing for you to come to him. And you thought this was the Christmas story.

I enjoy listening to a good band, a good orchestra and a good musician. I've learned to listen differently. An individual musician can play so well that you don't realize how many notes it takes to play one song. But it takes each note in a particular order to play any song. Then when you add other instruments, wow. As each instrument joins in and plays its part, the song becomes even more beautiful. When an orchestra plays, if you listen hard, you can distinguish the different instruments playing different notes. Playing their own parts in a very orderly manner. Now when they are warming up it sounds like noise and chaos. But when they play together, it's amazing. Now go play your part. Play it well. Play at the right time follow the conductor (Jesus). He will show you your part. Let's go make beautiful music together.

It is easy to see God in nature. In the things we can see and touch. We have His word and it is true. Every word, every dot. By faith we must believe in His greatness, His power, the constant salvation that He offers us. It's up to us to trust Him.

I woke up this morning wondering who I was. Not my name, but just who am I. I can see my whole body except for my face and my back. I know my thoughts. I know my intentions. I am so imperfect in every way. I can only see my reflection or image and the fruits of my actions. I can look in the cleanest mirror and still yet, it is only a reflection of who I am. I can see my shadow, but it is only an image.

God didn't build my body with the intention of me physically looking at myself in the face. Why I wondered. My theory is, we can look in the face of someone we know well, someone we have known from birth and yet still be wrong about them. Because we can't see their heart, their soul. We can only see the fruits of their actions. So as much as I claim to know me, what I can do? What I can accomplish? I really don't know me at all. But the one who created me, He knows me. He sees me inside and out. Nothing is hidden from Him. With him I have no secrets. Even though I try to hide things from him, the things that aren't good. He asks me for them and slowly, I give in. My Jesus can look at me and He knows who I am. Yet He still loves me. He's never given up on me. Even when I wanted to give up on myself.

Now, why can't I physically see my backside? I have a theory about that too. My backside represents everything that is behind me. The only way I can see behind me is by looking in a mirror and seeing a reflection. I can't even see the backside of my shadow. Behind me is my past. It's not to be relived, even the good moments. Trying to see my backside without a reflection just causes me to go in circles. Who needs that? Not me!

Going in a circle means going nowhere, right? And a mirror can only show a reflection of who I am, so my past isn't the now me, it's the past me. It's who I was. My today represents a new me. Every morning I wake up I have an opportunity to be who my Savior wants me to be. Every morning I wake up, I have the choice to follow Him, to represent Him or not. Today, I choose Him. I will leave my backside behind me and move towards the goal that Jesus has set for me. I heard that a very wise man said this, "Not my will, but your will be done."

May God reveal himself to you today:) It may be on the phone, at the store, in the doctor's office. Maybe He will reveal himself to you in the quiet of the morning or in the chaos of the day. Maybe He will reveal himself through the smile of a stranger, a song on the radio or a word from a friend. Keep your eyes open. Be kind and be ready. Represent Jesus well. You may be the one He reveals Himself through today.

33 years old and His time was ending fast. So He cherished every moment and made every minute count. Growing up in small towns, fishing with friends, going to weddings and funerals, going to church and to school was what everyone knew about Him. He wasn't the kind of guy that really stood out in a crowd, until He spoke. He was passionate about the things He knew.

You see, it had been a long time since anyone was passionate about God. In fact God hadn't spoken to anyone in four hundred years. So most just lived life by the law. Don't do this and don't do that. Keep this clean, throw that away. Don't touch this and don't touch that. Don't talk to them, don't go there. He was different, even as a pre-teen He was passionate about going to church and when it was His turn to read, He caught every ones attention. It wasn't just words to Him, It was more and even the teachers were awe struck at his knowledge and understanding. The love He had was incomparable with any others. He didn't just love His mother and His family, He loved everyone He met. He befriended those that were pushed to the side. He focused his attention on those others thought were trash. He was so different, so very different. At thirty He left home and started traveling, going from place to place, sharing his compassion for people and his passion for God. Showing everyone He talked to, the truth about God.

The church had all but turned into a courtroom. To Him loving God was more important than following traditional laws. Laws that men had put in place. He tried over and over again to tell them, but few were actually listening. The few that did, joined with Him in his travels. He shared precious revelations with them, told them secrets, poured His everyday life into them. He lived his life intentionally, focused on where He was going and what He was doing, though He would take time out of a busy life to share himself with this one or that one.

They say that all He had said and done could never have all be written down. His calendar was full 24-7. Out of all that knew of him and all that walked with Him, a book was written. It's an amazing book. Full of love, drama, war and peace, life and death. It starts with a void and ends with an amazing fullness. My Jesus, our Jesus, came to share all He knew about God first hand. He had seen Him with His own eyes. No other who spoke God's word had seen the beginning of the world. No other was God in flesh.

Have you been too busy to share your passion for Jesus with others, or has your passion been covered up with shame and guilt. Have you been compassionate or has your compassion been tainted with bitterness and hatred. If so, pray ask for forgiveness and get it back. This world needs Jesus. Don't hide your light under a basket full of pride, but share your light with others. Don't be afraid to love or be loved. I mean if Jesus loves you, can't He love them too. Remember, your time is ending fast as well.

Remember today how BIG your God is. There is nothing impossible for Him to do. He promised to never leave us or forsake us, but to be with us every moment of our lives. Remember?

As long as we have adults and children attending school and as long as they love Jesus and put him first, God will never be put out of schools. I think it's time we (including me) start acting like we believe in a God who is alive, a Jesus who forgives, a Holy Spirit that continues to convict us of sin. To begin to admit we have been wrong and are willing to let Jesus Christ change us. There are a lot of people who claim God isn't allowed somewhere. But I am here to tell you there is no such place on earth. He is allowed anywhere. He can be anywhere, at anytime, all the time, at the same time. He is omniscient and omnipresent. He isn't bound by man's rules. Never has been, that's why they killed Jesus, you know. He wouldn't abide by traditional, man endorsed laws. He healed on the Sabbath, He told the truth about God and His love. He embarrassed those who were suppose to know the scriptures. He wouldn't bow to Satan then and He sure isn't going to now. If Jesus Christ LIVES in you, then everywhere you go, He is there. There may be places that it seems like God isn't there and Satan would like us to believe that. But it isn't true. You can't tell me God created something He isn't allowed to be in. I believe that God is revealed in more schools than He is in some homes. Sorry for my rant..... wait, no I'm not.

What words would you say to change the life of another? Would you give them words of hope? Would you tell them to never give up? Would you encourage them? Does the life you live back up the words you would say? I truly do love Jesus. I believe He died for me, but I will admit, I don't act like it sometimes. There are days that I feel so defeated and then there are days that I feel as if I could conquer the world for Christ. Why? Are Christians ever allowed to feel this way?

Hmm, I believe even the disciples had their moments. So I do what they did. I have to encourage myself in the Lord, tell myself to never give up. I remind myself to hold on to the hope that Jesus gave me. That Jesus died for me and He loves me. I have to remind myself to share this hope with others, not just in word, but in my character and in my actions. I am a disciple of Jesus Christ, though I may not be bold as Peter, as brave as Paul, I have the same Savior. I have the same Holy Spirit that guided them, guiding me and I know I can't live a Christian life without Him.

We have an amazing God!! When He gives you a job to do, not only will He provide the job, but He will provide the talent, the passion and the ability to do it. All you need to do is obey. This coming year is going to be a year never to be forgotten. Some will blame the economy. Some will give praise to a man. Some will believe the lie and others will stand on the promise. Our God didn't promise us mansions on earth, nor did He promise great popularity of men. What He did promise was hope in a life eternal and a joy filled with peace in the midst of any circumstance. I'd rather have Jesus than silver or gold. I rather be His than have riches untold. I'd rather have Jesus than houses or land. I'd rather be lead by his nail pierced hands.

It is Sunday morning! Yippee. It's five degrees outside. Now that's cold. Of course cold is only the absence of heat. Darkness is just the absence of light. Death is just the absence of life. So if you are in a cold, dark, lifeless place, then I know just what you need to do. Find Jesus. He is the light that can chase away the darkness. His love can warm your heart and He will give you life everlasting!

Sometimes we need reminded..... Jesus loves the imperfect and the stubborn. He loves the tender, the bold, the simple and the complicated. He loves the rich, the poor, the middle class. He loves you and He loves me. It doesn't matter to him what our background is, where we have been or where we are at. He loves us enough to change where we are going.

I was blind, but now I see and I keep on seeing. I was deaf, but now I hear and I keep on hearing. I was a mute, but now I speak and I keep on speaking. I was lame, but now I walk and I keep on walking. I was lost, but now I am found and my salvation continues. Some of the greatest miracles that have ever happened to me. No I may not have been physically blind, deaf, mute. lame or lost, but spiritually (which is worse) I was.

Blind to the fact that I needed Jesus and relationship with Him. I was deaf to what His word was telling me. I didn't speak of His love to others. I had so much pride. I thought walking with the Lord was for wimps or (just the opposite) people who weren't afraid of anything, which was not me. What I found was this. We all need Jesus. He can open anyone's eyes to see the awesomeness of His love and power. He can open any ear that wants to truly hear the truth about God. He can stir up a fire in your innermost being that you can't help but share His love with others. But I also found that it's not only speaking but it's walking it out. Now do I feel his closeness every day? Sadly, no. So then I wonder what happened. Why can't I feel his presence every moment? Why can't I walk this life out without failure. Why do I let guilt eat me when I have fallen? Flesh, it's just flesh.

But someday, when I put this flesh aside, I will be perfect. When I leave this flesh on this earth, I will be complete. But until then, I must know my enemy. I must know his antics and recognize them.

"So Lord continue to open my eyes to see you, to open my ears to hear you, to open my mouth to speak what you would have me say and move me. Continue to show your love and grace to me when I fall and give me strength to get back up and try again."

I don't want religion, I want a relationship. I don't want just words, I want inspiration. I don't want wealth or power, I want Godly wisdom to know how to use what I have for His glory. There are enough rich and famous, there are enough geniuses, there enough religious people. There are enough people who just want to "hear" the word of God. It's time we become His hands and His feet. God is looking for the "willing". Remember He knows your intentions, He knows your weaknesses, He knows everything about you. And you are exactly what He's looking for.

All I know is that I was blind, but now I can see. The Good news isn't I am a bad person going to hell. The Good news is, I am a bad person that has been forgiven. On my own I cannot be good. On my own I am sill bad. On my own I can't live up to a right way of living. So I am becoming dependent on the one who is good, who is able to keep me, who can show me how to live. God is able.... Jesus did it..... the Holy Spirit reveals it...

Hanging out with Paul this morning, reading some 1 Corinthians. I really think He was talking to me. As mature as

I would like to think that I am, I am still a baby. Going around crying and whining because I did not get my way. Being loud because I am not happy. I want this, I want that. They didn't. They wouldn't. Fact is, this isn't behaving like a mature Christian, it's being a "carnal" baby. Paul was speaking to believers of all ages, of all backgrounds and he told them all, you are big babies.

Get over not getting your way. Go ahead take pride in all your works, go ahead. They're going to get put through the fire. It doesn't matter how precious they are or how simple they are. It doesn't matter if everyone boasts about you or looks down on you. Your works are going to be burnt. Those that make it through the fire are good, those that don't, well just be glad you survived the flames yourself. Remember, fire leaves a mark, burnt places, ashes and a stench. A mature believer in Christ Jesus will have a spiritual smell about them because they have been through the fire. May your boasting be in the Lord and not in men.

It doesn't matter what the name is of your church.
What matters is who is the owner of your heart.

To spend one moment, one breath with God...
It can change your life eternally.

It's Friday!! I'm glad Jesus loves me, even on the not so good days. You may say you love Jesus. That you are a Christian. Remember it's a relationship. If you are doing all the talking and all the asking then maybe you need to check your relationship. Jesus is by far the best listener I have ever met. But when He talks to me... It's life changing.

Everyday is an opportunity for God to do something
amazing in your life. Keep your eyes open. You don't
want to miss it. It's so easy to let things in this life
distract you. Keep your mind on the things above. Put

**to death sin and put away all bad attitudes, backbiting
and let the purest love of Christ dwell in your heart.**

Forget it. Quitting is not an option. Surrendering to my Savior
is all I can do. His will, His purpose. Give it all or go home. He
promised me, that I would not go thru anything that He and I
can't handle together. He promised to never, ever leave me (even
when I feel alone). He promised heaven was real. All I can do is
trust Him, follow Him, serve Him and love Him with all my heart,
mind and soul.

Living a life worthy to be called a follower of Jesus Christ
isn't easy. In fact it's impossible unless you have a relationship
with Jesus himself. The Holy Spirit is a great relationship builder.
Always leading and pointing to Christ and He uses not only words
of God, but the power of God to guide you.

Satan knows I'm up, so it's time to get my gear on and get
ready for a rumble. I know our enemy best when I am closest to my
Savior. My enemy's schemes stand out more, his plans get revealed.
And I know that no weapon formed against me, will prosper. That
doesn't mean my enemy isn't going to shoot. It doesn't mean he
won't hit his target, (my heart). It means even if, or when, I get hit
and I am wounded even to the point of death, my soul is secure
and all I have given my Savior (family, friends), He will take care
of to the end. So see his weapons won't prosper. They won't grow.
It won't cause me to fall away. He can't kill me. So I will run my
race, fight my fight, make my move (God's timing of course). I
won't give my enemy an inch or a moment of my time. Stand and
fight, the good fight. Now, let's hit it and hit it hard.

A beautiful day is approaching. Our God is amazing. The signs of spring are quickly being revealed. I love it. Brown grass, colorless trees, empty bushes, empty flower beds are beginning to show signs of life. Truly one of my favorite reminders about life. As one flower fades and dies, another will soon fill that empty place.

Live your life in such a way that you leave a good place for the one behind you. The legacy you are leaving behind may have started badly, but it can end with honor and praise. Few remember the flower that never bloomed, but they do remember the one that open up, and fill the air with a wonderful fragrance and amazing beauty.

No matter where or when I read the word of God, the gospel of Jesus Christ, it always says the same thing. Jesus loves me. I cannot just believe it, but I must also accepted His love. My life will change for the better. He knows my name and He calls me his own.

It's Monday. The battle is on. It's time to be a follower of Christ, not an actor of Christ. Actors only pretend to be someone else for a short while, or until something happens that throws them out of character. An actor expects to receive something for doing nothing. A follower, follows and imitates who he is following.

His character is being built daily. His eyes are focused on the one that is leading. A follower observes the leader, his intentions and after a while, knows the leaders heart. Even when a follower gets sidetracked and turns a wrong way, he knows where the leader is going, finds his leader and gets back on track. Stay on track. Jesus has given us many promises. To never leave us, nor to forget us or lead us on a wrong path. Stay true to God, whole heartedly. Even when you are among those that don't follow him or believe in him.

Love is long suffering and is kind. We know Paul was talking to believers. I know I am not very long suffering and I know I am not always kind, especially when I am suffering. Make today a day to be kind. No matter what comes your way, no matter what someone says or does. This includes you, being kind to yourself.

After reading, I believe I have been a clanging cymbal. All the spiritual things in my life mean little if I don't have love. If I am blessed with all kinds of gifts, but I don't love, it doesn't count. If I have every spiritual gifting healing, prophesy, knowledge, etc., it means nothing if I don't have love. May God reveal His love through me, because my love just isn't strong enough.

It's Sunday!! I get the honor of greeting people that enter church doors this morning. So exciting! Some are people I have known for years, some are visitors. I know that worship and listening to the preaching should be my favorite part, but I get mine during the week as well. Not just from going to church, but by having a relationship with my Jesus. So when I get the chance to say, good morning :) while standing at the door shaking a hand, giving a hug, letting someone know that "someone sees them and cares", well, that is just the icing on the cake for me.

Jesus tells me He loves me. Not just through His word, but through His people. Have you told Jesus you love Him, by loving someone else today? Too often broken hearts walk around and feel like they are invisible, uncared for, unloved. Funny, the ones we tend to not see, are the ones Jesus longs to have a relationship with. I once was blind, but now, I can see. Jesus is a mender of broken hearts, a companion to the lonely (even in a crowded room). He's a healer of the sick (not just physically but mentally). He disciplines those He loves, only to make us better and stronger. He can fill a hungry heart and a satisfy a famished soul. Do your best to get in "His" presence today. Turn the world off for a while (it's way too distracting).

What a wonderful day! Monday. Many say they don't like it. Well I do. I like the people I work with, I like what I do. I like waking up, getting into the word of God. God has given me a life to live and I am going to live it. Not with an evil heart, but a heart that rejoices because it has been forgiven. It is well with my soul....

Today let your focus be on pleasing a heavenly Father. He is pleased when we do good, when we submit to His authority and the authorities that He has set in place and in motion. His will is to reveal Himself to us, sometimes, it's through trials. Sometimes it's through evil kings and lords. Sometimes it's through His word and His presence.

When you are put in a dark room without any light at all, you can't see. You can't see how big or small the room is. You can't see if there are obstacles in your way. The complete darkness becomes a close wall all around you. When you MEET Jesus, you receive a small flashlight that can put off some of the darkness. So therefore you can see slightly the size of the room, the obstacles, in your way. But never the whole room at the same time. But if you ACCEPT Him as being the one in charge of your life and you trust Him, the light that has been in the room the whole time comes on. It illuminates the entire room. You can see it all clearly, every corner at the same time. Only then do you realize, how small the room really is and only then can you find the door that leads to freedom in Jesus. Are you in the darkness and need a light? Jesus is the light of the world! He dispels all darkness.

He knows your love for Him. And He knows that your love has human limits. He also knows you better than you know yourself. He wants to teach you the right way to love. Not with money or things. Not with flesh on flesh. But God with man. Jesus Christ the only perfect example of the truest kind of love. His love comes with adventures and trials. His love burns away the chaff (fake) love, His love can do exactly what you are searching for..... Give you hope, peace, satisfaction and you will "know" you are truly loved.

Reading in the OT this morning. God has always been good. His word is as real today as it was when He first spoke it. I used to be that someone that wouldn't read these books, on the grounds they weren't for today and I just didn't understand what they were saying. I did what I was supposed to do. Not out of love, but tradition (that's what mom and dad did). S o why would anything make sense to me? But now I see them as love letters, letters of warnings, letters with directions.

I have some things I personally am trying to give to God. It's not easy. It's my weaknesses, my own thoughts and ideas. It's what I expect for my life. You see, this life isn't easy, especially with so many distractions. I know God is working things out in my life. Not because I am righteous, but because He is. Good things don't come to me because I am good, they come because He is.

Walking by faith.... It's an action. Sometimes life is very clear and you can see the road that is laid before you. Sometimes life is unclear. We become blinded by things, by circumstances, by hopes and by dreams. When we take our eyes off of the goal, we forget about the race. We get confused on what the real prize is. The road of life gets foggy. When you get in a place where you just don't know what to do...... walk.

Re-focus your eyes, re-focus your mind and don't sit, don't run, but walk. In but a moment, you will feel Him walking beside you. He won't push or pull, but He will hold you, guide you. He didn't say life would be easy. He didn't say that at all. What He said was He would never, ever leave you. He said "Follow me."

There are so many voices that are speaking into our daily lives. Television, family, friends, wants, desires, etc. It gets hard to hear Him. Put away those things that distract you. Remove those things that cause you to turn away. Make that time, take that moment, to quiet yourself and listen.... When you can't hear His voice, when you can't feel His presence, have faith and walk. Follow Him.... by just doing what He said to do.

I've been in Deuteronomy this whole week. Moses can't go any further. He can only see what was promised but God said "only look, you can't enter. They have to go without you. Tell them these things... Love me, obey me, serve me with everything. Don't fall into thinking the way the world does. Don't do what they do!! They let their eyes see what they want. They let their hearts lead them to lies. They listen to lies and try to make them truths. They do not follow the same rules. But you are mine and I am yours. If you want things to go well with you, if you want my blessings, if you want my attention.... Listen to me!"

I have a cheap candle. I probably got it at Wal-Mart. I bought it because I liked the smell, it matched my colors and it was pretty. I have tried to light it in the past, but it wouldn't stay lit. Today, because I was home, I thought I would light it. Yep, just like before burns for a couple of minutes then goes out. But today was different. I dug out the wick and noticed the wick kept falling over into the melted wax thus putting out the flame. I wondered how many times I would have to dig it out and light it. Five times I dug that wick out and five times I lit that candle.

Cheap candle, the wick is crooked so it's not perfect like the other candles. Maybe I should just get another one, one that works. I have decided I am keeping this candle. I am going to light it as often as I can. Why? Because it reminds me of me. God just keeps digging me out straightening me up and lighting me on fire to burn for Him. Hmm how many times has He done that? How many times will He continue to do that? I have a feeling it will be as often as needed. I am glad He doesn't give up on me.... By the way my candle is still lit. All it needed was time.

I can't be fake around God. He knows when I'm pretending. He knows when I am lying. He knows the promises that I make, I won't keep. So why does He continue to forgive me? It's not because I am righteous. It's not because I am holy. It's not because I am famous, beautiful or smart. It's not because I am poor or rich. It's not because of anything I've done or promised to do. He loves me, and there's no other reason. Knowing you are truly loved, is the most freeing, motivating, most satisfying place to be. Let someone know they are loved. Not just by you but by a God who completely understands and unconditionally loves them. I know It makes me want to be a better person.

In a land full of giants? Ever feel that way? Things have gotten out of control. Circumstances are too overwhelming. All you see are failures, sicknesses and poor attempts. This world is full of giants. God prepared David to fight his giant. If we will listen and obey, God too has prepared us to fight ours. Sometimes we forget and try to fight without God. As David stood before his giant he spoke some very powerful words. "Hey giant, you've come to me with death and destruction, fear and defeat, but I come to you in the name of The Lord. I come to you in confidence that with the leading and strength of my God I will win. I come against the fear of death with the joy of life. I come against your destruction with the blessings of God. I come against defeat and claim victory. Victory not in my name, but in the name of my God." Giants come and giants go, but our God is mightier than all.

I have a good God. I have an amazing Savior.

Seems we struggle with such a simple task. Blessings follow obedience. Serve The Lord today, give him all your heart, all your soul and all your mind. No matter the task that is set before you, include Him in it. Remember His promises.

Yesterday on my trip to Paducah, I told my daughter about my favorite animals. No they aren't dogs and cats (surprise). They are eagles and sheep. The Bible speaks about these animals so often, that I can't help but want to learn more about them. The strength and majesty of an eagle and the dependency and meekness of a sheep. The life lessons you can learn from both of these animals is worth researching.

I would love to mount up on eagles wings. To soar above the storms, to fly high above every circumstance and problem. To see them for what they really are and know they are small compared to God. But what I am is a sheep. Completely dependent upon my Shepherd. Though sometimes unwilling to follow, though sometimes forgetful of where I am and where I am going, I am still a sheep. My shepherd has carried me on his shoulders, but not before I was broken. Yes, only the broken get carried. But in that brokenness comes "the knowing". Knowing who my Shepherd is, knowing his voice above all others, knowing his scent, his movements.

Few want to be broken, few want to admit that they have been or can be broken. Without brokenness, you don't need Him. You don't need a Savior. Even an Eagle, as great and mighty as they are, come to a time in their life where they must choose. Choose to be broken or die. An eagle, when it gets to the middle of its life, must choose a very painful process or death. It's beak has become so big it can't eat. It's talons have become so long it can't kill. It's wings have become so heavy it can't fly. It's choice is to die or remove them.

Removing them, they become vulnerable to other animal. They can even become prey. But choosing not to remove them is certain death. A miserable death and a short life. So they pluck their heavy feathers. They pullout their long talons and they bang their beaks on rocks to break it off. It's painful and it's dangerous. Their brokenness is their only hope. But then comes the healing. The feathers, the talons, the beak begins to grow. Life starts again... Not just any life, but a new one.

Right after His last meal, He knew He had to do something different. Something memorable. So He takes off His coat, removes everything that isn't necessary, gets a towel, some water and looks at His men. He loves them and He wants them to understand something. He kneels in front of each of them. Taking a gentle hold of their dirty feet, He washes them and dries them. They were astonished. What is He doing? He is too important, to highly esteemed. For goodness sake, He's going to take over Israel.

Coming to one of his closest friends, He calls him the Rock. The Rock refuses. He refuses because he didn't want his Lord to wash his feet. The Rock should be washing his Lords feet. But gently He talks to him and washes his feet as well. When He finishes, He puts away the dirty towel, throws away the dirty water and teaches them a very important thing. He said, 'You may call me Teacher and Lord, and you are right. So if I willingly wash your feet, if I your Lord bow my knee to do the dirty job, if I love you enough to touch you and wash you, then I want you you do the same. To love each other as much as I have loved you. No one is higher than the other. The one who was sent is not greater than the one who sent him. Love each other and you will be blessed."

It's hard to put pride aside. In fact it's nearly impossible but we have been told to do so. Love someone enough today, to put aside your own thoughts and feelings, your own wants and desires. It not only shows a Godly love, but proves it.

Decide what's worth fighting for. Then stand your ground and fight. Jesus focused on life not death. Choose this day who you are going to serve. God or something else.

Isn't it amazing that you can be sitting in the midst of stench and never know it until you leave and then return. Sin works the same way. The longer you sit in or around it, the less it bothers you, the less you notice it and the more you accept it. So, how do you get out of the stench if you don't know you are in stench? It's revealed to you. Not only by man, but by God. Suddenly, you realize...you're dirty and stink. My Father reveals my stench sometimes to me. Sometimes, those who care enough and love me enough, to tell me. Yelling at me about my stench has rarely worked, but a silent whisper gets me every time. Thank you Lord for revealing my stench (my sin) to me. Wash me, spray me with Your everlasting love and kindness. Help me to love those who are lost in their own stench and share your love with them, so that they too, will begin to sense their own smell and want you to wash them clean.

"Blessed are the poor in spirit for theirs is the kingdom of God." I don't think He means they don't have enough spirit, or that they have less than everyone else. I don't think He means they don't have enough to get by. Jesus spoke then and speaks now to us. Then face to face, now through His word. He spoke to them, encouraging them to not give up. The "holy roller spirit" isn't what gets you...into the kingdom. It's a heart that wants a relationship with him, more than anything. It's the spirit that isn't happy with earthly things, but longs for eternal treasures. Knowing that there is more to God than where I am, makes me realize I am poor. It isn't easy to "want" to read the Bible, but when you get a taste of it, you can't help but want more.

One of the easiest scriptures to find, and to me is also one of the most intriguing scriptures in the bible, is Genesis 1:1. "In the beginning God created the heavens and the earth." Some just read this verse and continue reading. But me, I see things a little different, it stops me, holding me there with awe and wonder.

The beginning. Think about it. What is the definition of "beginning"? Webster says it's the place where something starts, the origin, the source. So God started something. He spoke it. He created the source, the original plan, the starting line. If He started it, then He was already here. Do you realize that God doesn't have a beginning and if He has no beginning then that means He has no end. Everything that is created has a beginning and it has an end. God created the heavens and the earth and the heavens and the earth will pass away, but one things remains, God.

It is hard to comprehend something like that. My life has a starting placed. It was hidden until God's appropriate timing of my birth. My death will be the same way. Hidden until God's appropriate timing. My death will come as swiftly as my life began. So now what to do with this space in the middle, this space we call life?

Once God spoke, the earth was formed, the light and darkness were separated, the air and water were set in place. It was the beginning of everything. We are all in this life together. We all hurt, all experience happiness, all experience anger, and pain. It is what we do with our lives that makes us all so different. What are you doing with your space, your life?

There are some that their life is short, almost non-existent. There are others that their lives last a much longer time. It seems we are remembered more by how we lived our lives than what we accomplished in our lives. Whether we have wasted it or used it wisely. I have wasted a lot of mine and not knowing when it ends, shouldn't make me sad, but it should drive me to do something with it. A wasted life is a life that has never touched another. Even at the moment of conception a child has touched a life, made a difference.

So for today, what are you going to do with your life? Make changes, make decisions for the better, make a choice to choose God over everything else? God gave you your beginning and only He knows when it will all end. He has given you the choice on how you will spend it. In the "beginning" God created..... and the story begins.

Sometimes I wish I was a great speaker, able to tell crowds of people amazing things about God. To lead them, show them the way to Christ. Sometimes I wish I could be the one to lay my hands on the sick and they become immediately well. That I could see miracles right before my eyes. Sometimes I wish that I was smart, that when I read Gods word, no matter the book, verse or chapter, that I understood it all. That my knowledge of God was way above where it is now.

Most of us has wanted one or all of these things. You know, to be recognized for something amazing, something rare, something life changing. In my reading this morning I have found I can have any or all of these. Isn't that awesome? Just one thing keeps me from receiving. You see, I can have faith that can move mountains. I can give everything I have away and seek only God and his wisdom and knowledge. I can even die for the gospel, and still not have the most important thing. Love. I come so short in this area. My love is limited and conditional. Read 1 Corinthians 13: 4-10. Read it slowly, pausing at the commas, stopping momentarily at the periods. Then ask yourself, search your heart, is that you? I found myself sorely lacking. Without love, I am nothing even if I have everything. Let God put His love inside of you. Let go of hurts and old dead dreams. Let God give you what you need for today and share it.

I hate every second you don't want me or need me in your life. Yet you say you "Love me". How do I know you love me? When I turn around a find you following me and doing what my Son told you to do. Love the Lord with all your heart and don't lean on your own understanding.

Trust Him, lean on Him and He will direct your paths. He will guide you through good times and bad times. He will pick you up when you fall. He will mend all that needs mending. He promised to never leave you, to never forsake you, to always be there. He's God. He is the only one who can make those promises and keep them.

Oh what a beautiful garden. Lush and green, smells of sweet aromas, lilac, roses, lavender. Mmmmm. Maybe this garden is full of sweet corn, green beans, tomatoes, peppers, etc. Either way a garden can be beautiful. Note "can be". A garden must be maintained, watered, plenty of sunshine, fertilized, weeds removed, rocks thrown out, bad bugs killed, good bugs encouraged. Then there is the tilling, keeping the ground soft and airy. It requires constant maintenance and constant attention. There isn't a day that goes by that something doesn't need or even require, to be done. A beautiful garden doesn't come easy, you can hire someone else to do it, but then it would be their garden, not yours. I have a garden. It's a secret garden filled with all kinds of things. It's not the kind you see with your eyes, but I must take care of it the same way. Just because it's in a hidden place, doesn't mean it's easy. In fact, it's harder.

The weeds, oh those weeds, some have very sharp and painful thorns and the roots go deep. Horrible rocks, who put them there? No matter how big or how tiny, they are annoying. Did I plant these weeds? Today's chore list, wear gloves, pull weeds, gather rocks, till the ground and water. Tomorrow pull weeds, gather rocks, fertilize, till and water. At the beginning of this garden, it was hard to tell the weed from the seedling. So I had to let both grow, but eventually I could tell the difference and separate them. My garden is my soul, my heart. It started off with some good soil, then sin entered(weeds (distraction), rocks (word killers), and hardness (lack of belief). But with constant care, and daily intervention with my Master Gardener, my garden will be full of good soil and will reap a great harvest. As awesome as all of this sounds, don't forget fertilizer. You know what that's made of, right? Crap, yes I said crap. Life is full of it. But in time and if used wisely, it can and will fertilize your garden and you will grow.

I must have my Master Gardener's help and His guidance to keep this garden in check. I could do it without Him, but then this would all get too over whelming. Today's chore list: Contact Master Gardener these weeds are choking me out....

We have an awesome God. From the beginning, God has used people that others would not "spit" on if they were on fire. He uses the rejected, the losers of this world to reveal His awesomeness, His greatness, His mercy and His compassion. Only one was ever born perfect. Only one ever walked this earth sinless.

So what's that mean? It means that you have a chance to be something in God's kingdom.... I have a chance. The refuse of this world has a chance to be great in God's kingdom. This weekend was absolutely what I needed. Surrounded by lost, sin stinking, filthy talking people that God loves more than I ever could. Watching his grace and mercy enter into their eyes as He captures their heart. Wow! God doesn't give up easily. He is definitely more patient than I am. Lives changing one by one. I love to see God moving, changing people, encouraging them and revealing to them what life is about.

Your body is made up from so many different members. There is the obvious head, arms, legs, hands, etc. There are parts that are made to be seen and parts that meant to be hidden. But all are parts of the body. Right? You have one body, yet when your toe hurts your whole body hurts and limps. You have one body, yet when your stomach is upset, your whole body is sick. Each body part depending on the other. Ever wonder? Why the body of Christ hurts?

We have His word and it is true. Every word, every dot. By faith we must believe in His greatness, His power, the constant salvation that He offers us. Jesus understands the "why". It's up to us to trust Him. Life with Him is so much better than life without Him. Wow. All I can say is God, you ARE good!

Reading God's word puts things into perspective. Our needs and our wants, can blind us and give Satan a place in our lives. Satan will encourage us to speak things that will feed our soul's pride and bitterness. Satan wants us to believe that he will allow us to have an easy life if we would just prove to him how "Christ like" we are. Satan will promise us all kinds of powers and gifts, if we would just bow to him and give him authority over our lives. It's so simple, it's the easy life, the road most traveled. I mean, if I can just say I want something, sign a paper and get it, is that bad?

What if I know God has promised me heaven, yet I choose to walk a life so close to the sin that I even smell like death? Is that pushing God to the limits? What if I accept all the blessings of men? What if I am promised good things in life and I promise to use them for good? Is that what God wants? Jesus was tempted with these things, yet He knew the most important things in life are not what we see with our eyes or touch with our hands, or even what others think about us. He knew then and knows now, the most important thing is putting God first in our lives.

It's an easy thing to say, but living it can put you at the bottom of the food chain. If something, anything, anyone, is between you and God, if it consumes your thoughts, takes your time, puts God on a back burner, then you are in dangerous territory. Find God and put Him first. Keep Him first, then your needs will be met, your soul will be satisfied, and your mind will be at ease. God is good and He wants the very best for you. Even if the very best means going thru terrible times (hell) to get there. You won't go alone, I promise.

God has given you an awesome day, now don't waste it on being selfish. It's human instinct to be selfish. So get rid of that "scent" by showering it with "love". We all know self has a problem, it wants its way all the time. So get rid of "self" and then you will be self-less. Someone who is in love has a tendency to be self-less. Jesus is in love with you and He has always been self-less.

Jesus is a life giver. From the moment He was placed in an earthly womb He has given hope and life. We are all going through phases in our lives. We were all born into sin, we have all turned away from Him. We have all failed. We have a past... that we are ashamed of. Whether it's playing a good person at church or being a rebel towards the kingdom of God. He loves you. He loves me.

We are loved by a God who is very jealous for us. Yes, He doesn't want to share you with worldly things. Every day He gives you and I the choice to follow him, to give us a better life. Not just for now but for eternity.

It's Monday. Each day goes by so fast. I am continually challenged to give up or give in. To surrender or run. To take a leap of faith or settle. Today I give in, surrender and leap into today and what God has planned for me. There is someone who needs to know that the law won't save them, Jesus will. That with Christ, a guilty heart can become guilt-free.

What a beautiful day my Lord has made. I'm going to go to church rejoice and then go outside and be glad in it. Some scriptures are to be taken literally, not just spoken

God speaks in such clever ways. Last night staring at the night sky, I noticed the moon and the stars and a scripture came to my mind, Genesis 1. In the beginning God created the Heavens and the earth.... I began to talk to God about it (in my own human interpretation) as I remembered it.

God, before there was anything there was You. You created something out of nothing. You separated the water from the air. You created the sun, moon and stars and you placed them each one in their specific place. You separated the night from the day. You told the seas and oceans where to stay, the mountains where to stand. You created the plants and animals and told them to re-create.

Then You decided to create something in your image, Your likeness. Something that could "choose". So You created man. Formed out of the dust, You breathed life into him. I can't even begin to imagine what that relationship was like. Then you asked

Your creation to give names to everything You had created, and He did. Then You saw the loneliness of man. Even though You walked with him, You knew that even then Your creation longed for something to be added to his life.

So You put the man into a deep sleep, opened up his side and removed a rib. From that rib, You created woman. Man and woman You created, created to choose to walk with You. Then it happened.... sin. The relationship was damaged and from that moment on, You have been trying to repair it.

Man's choice is just that, man's choice. You could have created man without a choice, but then, man would be like the angels, beings without choice. That's not what You wanted. You wanted a relationship with someone who would "choose You". To choose You over everything else. But sin damaged that choice, man's choice. Your choice has never changed. Your choice has always been, from the moment You created man, to have a close relationship with him.

It was not your fault, God. It was man's. It was mine. Yet, You still choose me even though my choices are as up and down as the waves in an ocean. Today, I choose you and maybe, just maybe, someone else will choose you too. Walk with me today, talk with me, share with me because I am Yours and You are mine. May your light shine in the ones that love You and reveal all that You are to those who don't know you.... yet.

Stir it up! That is my thought this morning. I can think about the wrongs in my life and become angry mad, bitter, because I stirred it up. I can think of sad memories and become sad or even depressed, because I stirred it up. I can think of happy memories, embarrassing memories, just by stirring it up. My memories are full of good and bad things just from living my life. I can choose everyday to stir any, or all, of them up.

The one thing I try to stir up every morning is the spirit of God that dwells within my heart and mind. Whether it is singing praises, speaking of Gods goodness and His love for me or whether it's reading His word or having a conversation with Him, I must start it up. My humanity would rather choose the other areas, but those roads lead nowhere good.

Timothy 1:6 says to stir up the spirit of God, by the laying on of hands. So I lay my hands on His word. I lay my eyes on my goal (heaven). I lay my troubles and burdens at His feet, surrendering them. I stir it up!! It is better than any alcohol I have ever drank. It is better than any drug I have been given. It is better than any counseling I have had. It is life to my spirit and food to my soul.

If you don't like your life, how things are going. If circumstances distract you and depress you, then STIR IT UP! God loves you. Jesus died for you and sent the Holy Spirit to fill you. Now it's up to you to fan the flames, stir that Godly gift, fight for your mind. Don't give up, stir it up!

It's Tuesday, the 3rd day of the week, it is the 322nd day of the year. There are 8 days until Thanksgiving, there is 34 days until Christmas, 41 days left of the year. Now that I've got your attention.... what are you going to do with the days that are left? Waste it complaining of all the time that has been wasted, freak out because time is flying by or are you going to make the rest of this year count? Be a blessing to someone every day. Love and be loved.

We all seek something that soothes our souls. The main ingredient is forgiveness. It's something we have a hard time receiving. As I was reading this morning a thought occurred to me. Do we have a hard time receiving forgiveness because we have a hard time forgiving? I am a grudge holder. When someone hurts me or someone I care for, it makes me mad. I can stay mad for a long time towards them, even if they don't know it. Whether it's intentional or not it doesn't matter. I justify it because it was wrong.

God's word says unless you forgive you won't be forgiven. That sunk in deep. Any good things I've done yesterday will not count if I let sin run my life today and saturate my tomorrow. Nor will my sins of yesterday, (if I stop doing them and ask for forgiveness for them), keep me from receiving eternal life. Your righteousness of yesterday will be forgotten if you fill your today and tomorrow with unrighteousness.

When someone does me wrong, I want them to pay. I want them to suffer. Do you get me? But God has a different view on this. He doesn't take pleasure in the death of an evil person. What? But God, they are mean and are against you. You should enjoy their removal from life. They don't deserve you. They haven't done anything good in life.

That isn't how God works, nor is it how we should be. God's quick to remind me that at one time I was that person and without Him I could be that person again. Pray, not just that they be forgiven and receive salvation, but pray that you receive the strength to forgive them. Why? It may be the one thing that keeps you from feeling that pure love, that unconditional love. It may be the reason you are stuck in life. It may be the reason you don't feel forgiven or maybe you can't forgive yourself. Gods pretty smart about this. He says to forgive and then you will be forgiven. So today I'm going to do just that, forgive. It won't be easy, but if I want to take this next step closer to my Savior, I must.

Today I get the awesome privilege of ushering at LCC. Some may look at it as a task or a duty. Not me. I look at it as a moment in time to hug a neck, tell someone good morning, show the love of Christ to everyone, and usher them into the house of God. When

I need God the most, I find Him best when I'm serving Him and loving His creation.

I would rather you be for Me or against Me. But instead, you claim to follow Me but live your life like you don't know Me. I see your heart, your intentions. I know your actions and your deeds. You have forgotten Me, but I have not forgotten you. I have never stopped loving you, but you forget I am jealous. I am jealous of the things that you love more than Me and because you love them, you can have no part of Me. I have stood by patiently waiting for you to notice, but you haven't noticed Me at all. I have filled your heart with a hunger for Me, but you fill your belly with things to forget Me. I won't wait for long, standing outside your door. But if you want to come back to Me. If you want to restore your love for Me, all you have to do is come to me with a broken heart, ready to change, call on my name and I will run to you. My name is Jesus. When you call me, I can be there faster than the blink of an eye or the last beat of a heart.

You are God and I am not. You have been teaching me to trust You from my youth. From my first memories, to this moment, You have known my future. The plans You have for me are for my good. Every brick laid in my life is building a foundation for my eternity. You love me beyond anything I could ever imagine with my human mind. I blame You, get angry at You, I run to You and reach out to You. You are my hope. You are my help when darkness surrounds me. You strengthen me for today and give me hope for tomorrow. You are God and I am not. May Your peace comfort all those who love You. May your love show through those who know You, through actions and not just words. Because You are God and I am not.

Not much hurts more than watching a loved one walk away. The urge to chase them, becomes intense. You know the path they are following and you know where it leads. Forgiveness has been given more times than it has been received.

Christ watched many walk away. They stated that His teachings were too hard. Many walked away before they ever knew Him. He didn't have the position in the government that they wanted Him to have. He didn't have the fancy home to live in. He didn't require special treatment or special honor or status that they wanted. He wasn't who they wanted Him to be.

He spoke of His father owning cattle on a thousand hills, yet never gave a cow to anyone. They walked away because they were looking through their eyes and not seeing with their hearts. What He was offering wasn't highly esteemed by them. They wanted recognition, position, wealth and power. All the way to Calvary, this is what many were waiting and expecting. When their expectations weren't appeased, that's when the truth about Him and who He was began to be revealed. The empty tomb, revealed a power they had never seen. The ascension and the promise gave hope that they had never felt. The Holy Spirit, gave strength and boldness like they had never experienced.

Have you walked away from Him? If you have, He has a great return policy. All returns are accepted, no matter the condition. Do you have loved ones that have walked away? Are you willing to walk this life alone for Him? His promises aren't fame and fortune, but peace and riches that go beyond this world. Pray for those who have walked away. Pray for their swift and safe return. Stay strong in who God wants you to be. Fight the good fight, run the race. Keep the faith. Endure every hardship. He promised heaven is worth it and I believe Him.

Don't you know you are worth more than silver or gold. Jesus knows the cost of every life. He paid for it. He did the very thing we could not do, pay the price for our sins. We may have to suffer the consequences but not the penalty.

We have all lost something. You're not upset because it's not replaceable, you're upset because it was yours. You've looked everywhere, searched everything, but still you can't find it. Where was the last time you saw it? When was the last time you had it in your hand? So you walk around in circles searching for something that will hopefully remind you of where it is. You go back to the places you were before, in hopes that it will be found. Losing something is as easy as dropping it, setting it down or walking away from it. A distraction can cause you to set it down with the intention of returning for it.

Do you remember the feeling of loss, once you find it? Not really, because the joy of finding it is greater than the pain of losing it. Though you do take better care of it than before. I've treated my relationship with God the same way. There have been days when I thought I was holding it close. You see it's my greatest treasure. Then along comes a circumstance of life. The distraction caused me to set it down, drop it and walk away from it. Once I realize I've lost it, the frenzy begins. Guilt, anger, bitterness all take their places. I look and search but my distraction is persistent, it won't let me go.

Then comes the thoughts of I'll just replace it. Deeper and deeper into sin I go. The guilt ridden feelings I have to drown out with, you got it, more sin. My life is out of control. Why? I quit looking. I quit searching. I settle for something temporary in place of something eternal. Then I come to a point... have I gone too far?

My Father says I can never go so far that He can't reach me. So I stop, turn and scream His name. He leaves the righteous ones and comes running to me. He picks me up, places me on his shoulders and carries me home. The joy is unimaginable. My joy for being found and His joy for finding me. I have my treasure back! Funny how I remember being lost, but my Father doesn't. He remembers the rejoicing. When I try to remind Him, He just points to the east and to the west and says, "It's as far from you as the east is from the west. Thrown into a sea of forgetfulness, I remember nothing, but I have joy because you are with me today." May the lost be found. May those who are searching find it. May those who are seeking never give up and may those who are knocking, keep knocking.

I was raised in church. Every Sunday morning, Sunday night and Wednesday night. Even more if there was a revival. I was taught bible stories, the Ten Commandments, how to pray, how to live a Christian life. My foundations were strong. Why would I walk away from it? A young man ran to Jesus wanting assurance of eternal life. "I have kept the 10 commandments from youth what else is there to do?" Jesus... said to him, "I know you know commandments, but there is something you lack." This young man sounds a lot like me. Raised living and breathing a Christian life. What could he lack? All the young man was searching for was eternal life. Just like me.

The lack? Sell everything and give it away. Then come follow me. Jesus loves this young man, but did this young man truly love Jesus? Too many responsibilities, too much stuff. Maybe he enjoyed his position in life. Jesus asked him to surrender and the young man walked away. Just like me. It doesn't say if later in this young man's life, he ever returned or what happened to him. Just that he walked away sad. He didn't get the answer he wanted. I've been there. I've gotten the answer I didn't want. Have you? I walked away too. But my story isn't over.

I loved you before this day every began. I loved you before you ever took your first breath. I loved you then and I love you now.

It doesn't matter what you've done. It doesn't matter who you are. I still love you.

My best friend doesn't judge me according to rules that I have kept or rules I have broken. My best friend has given up everything for me and in turn has given me everything. It breaks my heart each time I hurt Him. I know the moment when I do it. I can feel it in my heart. He tells me He loves me and He forgives me The most amazing thing is, I know it. Even on the days I don't feel like I deserve it. His Father calls me His own, He calls me daughter. Because of my best friend, I have hope for tomorrow, even if tomorrow doesn't look very hopeful. He loved me then and He loves me now. Someone needs to know that. There is someone who loves you, someone who has loved you back then and loves you now. There is someone who cares about your today and your tomorrow.

Jesus spoke pretty harshly to the Pharisees. They must have been watching every move, listening to every word, critiquing everything that Jesus and his disciples were doing. Don't you just love it when... people do that. Believe me, you can never do anything right under such scrutiny. Jesus and the disciples were about to eat. They had been with sick people all day. Touching them and being touched by them. Instead of focusing on the miracles of the day, the Pharisees focused on the fact that the disciples didn't wash their hands in the proper Jewish traditional way. Using special water from special pitchers. Good grief.

Have you ever felt that way? You did it, it got done, but someone is angry because you didn't do it their way. It wasn't Gods law, it was man's tradition. Man's tradition gets between man and God a lot. Jesus stepped up and told them they were wrong. He told them that they have disobeyed Gods laws too many times to follow a law made by man. Laws that they put in place. Laws that they thought was respecting God. They followed rules, to the T, but they disobeyed God easily with their hearts. Jesus told them it isn't the food or water you eat that makes you unworthy to worship God. It's the things you say and the things you do that make you unworthy. I can drink dirty water and it doesn't make me dirty. It isn't beneficial for me and it might make me sick, but it doesn't make me dirty. What makes me dirty is the evil thoughts, pride, foolishness, wickedness, an evil eye, and there are plenty more. (Check our Mark 7.) Those come from the heart, the spirit of a man, not from the belly.

God forgive me for being lazy and not searching your truth. Honoring You is much more important than anything else in my life. May my life honor You. May my life turn people towards You and not away from You. You are holy and deserving of a holy life. Forgive me for being a Pharisee, forgive me for putting mans thoughts and ideas above Yours. Lead me in your truth, so that I may follow You closer today than I did yesterday.

It isn't about me. In my own strength I am nothing. In my own wisdom I am a fool. But with Christ everything is possible.

Today you can change a life. Today you can save a life. Today is a new beginning for someone. Remembering what used to be and dwelling on yesterday, will only benefit you today if you learned from it. Everyday God's mercies are new. He didn't promise that you wouldn't have bad days, He promised when you had one He would be with you. Keep your eyes open. Seek what wonders He has in store for you. You may just be surprised that the life that gets changed is yours.

Which is better? Option One: To listen to some one tell you the fire is hot and if you touch it you will get burned. Or Option Two: See fire, feel heat, touch it and get burned? Most of us live our life choosing option two. We have heard option one repeated several times, but we either didn't believe or weren't listening to the person sharing this with us. Throughout the bible we receive information about things we should stay away from, avoid, walk away from, run from. But yet when these things get close to us we don't listen to or choose not to remember the instructions on staying away from it.

Listening is the beginning of wisdom. The fire is hot. But understanding and using the knowledge that the fire isn't bad if used correctly and you learn how to use it. Lacking wisdom, understanding or knowledge, will give you a very painful blister. Life is this way as well. The bible doesn't say we won't have trials or troubles or ever have to deal with wickedness. What it does say is when they do come, keep your eyes focused, not leaning to the right or the left, but looking straight forward. Eyes on the target, Heaven. Choose to remember Godly instruction. Choose to follow the path that Jesus Christ left for us. Choose to listen to those who know how to use fire correctly. In doing this, you can have a wonderful meal, a warm home, and a lamp to see through the darkness.

I've been wondering about the term "normal". I've said it and heard it most of my life. "All I want is to have a normal life. What is it that we base being "normal" on. Comparing our lives to the lives of others? Some on TV, some at work, some at church. What do you believe normal is? Life without problems? Life with all the money and things you could ever want? A life on a deserted island away from everyone? We drive ourselves to crazy points in life in search of what we refer to as normal. Yet those who seem to have a normal life aren't happy. They live in ruts.

God didn't intend for us to live "normal" lives, but lives full of life in a search for Him. Life has it has ups and downs, it has life and death, it has hopes and dreams. Quit looking for "normal". Look for Jesus Christ in every moment of the life you are given.

Quit wishing you had a different life. If the life you are living isn't pleasing God, change it. If the Christian life you are living isn't pleasing you, search your heart. God isn't finished with you. Pray, read, talk to Him. No one else can make you happy. Only God can truly make you happy with yourself. Jesus loves you. That should be enough. It's a promise you can live on and die with.

God's timing is everything! Every promise ever given was given according to His timing. From the beginning, to Isaac, to John the Baptist, to Jesus. His life, His death and His resurrection. His promise to return is still yet to be, but it will take place in God's timing.

Your promises are according to your timing, your ability, and your will. We fail at our promises because our timing is usually off. Too late or too early. God's timing is perfect. Though we get disappointed at God's timing, when we look back we realize just how perfect it really is.

No matter what you are going through, it is not hopeless.

Who does this guy think He is? I've seen him before going into the church. In fact I've listened to him. He's good. He can keep my attention. Just the other day He rode into town with horns honking and people shouting. People were standing on the side of the road celebrating like the president was in town. Then He went to the church and just stood there looking around. What's up with that? Then He left town quietly. When He came back to town the next day, He came in quietly. But wow! He went to the church and had a fit. He told people to get out!! What a temper He has. I guess He was tired of all the games being played at church. Then He sat down and began talking to those that stayed. It was great watching people try to "catch" him in a lie or try to "stump" him with questions. I loved it. He didn't shake. In fact, I think maybe

He was annoyed at their lack of knowing anything, but acting as if they knew all the answers. First was the religious people, then came the government, then came more religious people. Funny, they thought they had him. He made them feel pretty dumb in front of everyone. They left mad. Scary mad. Then as if nothing had happened He began to talk to us again. He said, don't be like that. Don't be walking around thinking you are better than everyone else. Don't put yourself above everyone else. When you do, someone will put you in your place, eventually. Church people tend to do that. Because we think we've "got this", we walk around acting as if everything is beneath us. Jesus was real with people. He was in the middle of their lives. He told them about God's kingdom and about sin. He told them He was leaving and that He would be coming back. He told them the truth. He wasn't lying. He wasn't just telling a fairytale story. He was preparing them.

He's preparing you and me for something better. Something more grand. Here, we will have troubles. But don't forget, He overcame every trouble, every disease, every terrible thing in life. Not for his benefit, but for yours. He is the Savior. He is the Son of God. They didn't believe He was. Who do you believe He is? What you believe about Him effects everything in your life.

We forget too easily the things we need to remember and remember too easily the things we need to forget. Those who don't read it, won't be able to understand it. Those who don't pray won't be able to retain it. Those who don't have a relationship with Him won't desire to read it. God's Word. Written for you. Not just for yesterday, but for today and tomorrow

What idol do you have? What is an idol? How do you know if it's an idol? Maybe these two questions will help.

1. An idol is something between you and God. If someone says anything about it, you become very defensive or secretive about it.
2. It is on your mind more than anything else. There is no limit or image that an idol could be. It can range from a job to your finances (extra money or no money). It can be from your children all the way to a church building. Sometimes "time" can be an idol, not enough of it.

God doesn't want anything between you and Him. Put God first every day, all day. Do a periodic check on your thoughts and your heart. Ask God to reveal those things that are your idol or idols. We may not like the answers, but if you want a closer walk with Him, it's required. The first of the ten commandments. Jesus spoke of it often. So do it. No whining, complaining, throwing a fit. Give it to God, period.

Sometimes we don't know how we get into such bad positions. But remember this... Jesus is able and willing to save you. But even better, He is willing and able to restore you. Not to where you once were, but closer to Him than you have ever been.

God has a plan. You can choose to be in it or not. To be a part of His plan, you must give up your own. Not an easy task, is it? It feels good to say, but in reality many fall because of it. Give up my plans, my will, to choose His? The twelve men closest to him struggled with it. Jesus in the garden even asked for it to pass, but said "not mine, Father, but yours". Be careful not to become prideful on where you stand in your Christian life. Be careful and watch yourself, it's too easy to choose your will and say it's God's will. Read His word, keep your relationship close with Him. Keep your eyes wide open. Put sin in its place, sometimes with love and sometimes with mercy.

When you book a flight, you must have a destination. When you get in the car, you need directions. Life is a lot like that. You need to find the point of your destination and set your life to go in that direction. My destination is Heaven. I must daily point my life in that direction to reach it. That doesn't mean there aren't bumps, pit stops, lay overs or changes of transportation. It may mean every now and then there is a change of altitude, a change of pace. But my destination is the same. I've been given the right directions and if I follow them closely, I'll get where I am going.

How is your relationship with Christ? Have you received the directions that He sent? Are you following them? If not, get back on track. Get back on the right road. There will be days when you will walk, others days when you will run. And there will be days when you will need to climb and it is all training you for the day you will get to fly.

What does it mean to be committed? What does it mean to be faithful? What does it mean to be in love? Everything. It means everything. I am a part of a very unusual group, the "Married and Still in Love with Each Other" group. I still enjoy weddings. The look of the grooms eyes when she, the bride, steps in. For a moment it takes his breath away. For a moment she stands there behind the door. A deep breath and then the door opens. The song and the journey begins.

For many, a marriage is a fairy tale with princesses and princes, kings and kingdoms. For some it's a compromise. If it doesn't work, it's just a divorce. For others, it's for life. It's meant to last until "death do us part." I've witnessed all three of these marriages. I've witnessed the dominating King or Queen who rules. I've witnessed the married now, divorced tomorrow. I've witnessed the ones who stood next to their husbands, who sat by their wife, while life slipped away.

Which one's were committed? Which one's were faithful? Which one's knew what true love was? Which one never had a fight, never had a problem, or never suffered a loss? None of them. All had problems. All had a fight. All suffered a loss. It's clear how much one loves the other, by the sacrifices that they make for each other.

The greatest sacrifice ever made, was given by an amazing Groom for His bride and the wedding hasn't even happened yet. The Groom is still preparing the home. The Bride is still preparing her gown. But soon both will be complete.

The Groom has been faithful, not once has another caught His eye. But the Bride? Well she has tried to remain committed to Him. She has tried to remain faithful. She has tried to love Him only. But her eyes keep searching for something better. She knows when the Groom comes, what He will be expecting. She knows she isn't ready yet. Time has caused her to become lazy. Time has left its mark on her. Compromise has stained her dress. Regrets has left it's ugly scars on her face and on her heart. Fear is gripping her mind.

This Groom is different from all other grooms, and she knows it. The wedding is soon and she thinks she has plenty of time. What will the Groom find when He comes for her? He still loves her, no matter what, He loves her. But his love for her doesn't keep her from falling in love with another. Her love for another will lead her away from the Groom. Her unfaithfulness will cause her to settle for the wrong groom, the wrong relationship.

I can honestly say sometimes, I really don't like what God is doing. I mean let's be honest. Sometimes love hurts. Sometimes our vision of what we want in life gets in the way of what God wants in our life. Sometimes I get angry when I see injustice happening and I know God sees it and I don't see him doing anything. Sometimes all I want is His blessings and all I get are trials.

Sometimes I want..... there it is, "I" rearing its ugly head again. Getting closer to him reveals the ugliness of my heart. It isn't easy to put "I" on the back burner. To make "I" not so important. When "I" is out of the way then "He" can work on me, change me, mold me. Nope, now that doesn't sound very comfortable does it?

Work, change, mold. Nope those three things sound painful and hard. But they are required to become more like Him. Jesus won't fit into my mold. He won't change to become like me. He would have to quit working to fit into my life. So I'm the one who needs to be worked on, changed and molded. I'm glad He doesn't make me do this alone. He's with me every step of the way. Now, "I" you just get out of the way today. It's not about you. It's all about HIM.

A worldly sorrow produces death. While a Godly sorrow produces repentance, leading to salvation that is not to be regretted. How do you know if you were made sorry in a Godly way? Godly sorrow produces diligence, clears away indignation against sin. It will create a fear of God, a driving passion for God and a want to make things right. Worldly sorrow produces depression, bitterness, hate, etc. Be sorrowful for the wrongs in your life, but make sure it is the right sorrow.

God woke you up this morning. He has a plan for your life. If you want to be involved in it, talk to Him. He specializes in taking a messed up life and using it for His glory.

My daughters must think that there is a fairy that cleans up their messes. They go to bed and dishes are on the table, dirty clothes in their rooms and they wake up to clean clothes and clean dishes. Hmmmm. Sometimes, I make them help me or even make them clean up their own messes when they wake up. God works that way too, doesn't he? We make a mess of our life, we call on His help, He makes things better. We mess it up again, call on Him, He makes it better. It's a terrible circle.

But sometimes, He says wait a minute. You're going to help this time. You made this mess. I watched you. You expected me to clean it up without you, again. Get your hands in here. You are going to get dirty with this one. I'll help you, but I'm not going to do it for you.

We face consequences of our messes. Oops. We weren't really expecting that one. Though He warned us, though He helped us many times before, we still wouldn't listen. Ouch. Consequences of bad choices are bad messes. That isn't the plan God has for your life, though it doesn't keep Him from using you, it does hinder the good you could have been doing. Start today, a new day, giving God first place in your life. Ask him to help you through each step of cleaning your messes. Remember, He didn't make it you did.

For God so loved everyone born on this earth that He sent His one and only Son to die for All of them. And anyone who believes in Him doesn't have to die but can have life forever. He took the punishment for your sins and died for them so you wouldn't have to. Even you at your worst, Jesus loves you. This will never change.

Which hurts more? Someone you love betraying you? People spreading lies about you? Being mocked by your peers or getting beaten by someone who hates you? The worst part is you haven't done anything. You're innocent. Those who are spreading lies, can't get their story straight. Those mocking you have no idea what you've been through. Those that are hitting you, do so for fun and to humiliate you. Those that betrayed you are the same ones you've given everything to. Wow, I think I've been there. My best friend hated me because we liked the same guy in High School. I didn't even fight for him. I just liked him and she knew it. She spread terrible lies about me, humiliating me. My own thoughts beat me up. My loneliness was almost more than I could bear. I didn't think I deserved it. I didn't think she would turn on me. As small as that moment in time seems right now, I still remember it.

How can I say Jesus doesn't understand? His heart was broken. He didn't want to go through all the pain mentally or physically. He didn't want to see with His own eyes, His best friends turn on him. He didn't want to hear with his own ears, "I don't know him." He didn't want to feel that disappointment, that loneliness that comes with the cross. But He did. He felt it through every strike of the whip. He saw it through every eye in the crowd. He heard it from the ones that just a few days ago were praising him, but now were cursing him, mocking him.

I'm so sorry Jesus. I didn't understand how much you really understood my pain, my loneliness. I have never experienced the pain you felt that day. Which hurt more? The nails or the touch of my sin? Did one distract you from the other? Jesus, I'm sorry. I didn't mean to push you aside. It's just I wanted them to like me. I was afraid. I was embarrassed. I was more concerned about what they thought, than what you thought.

Jesus forgive me for my failures of yesterday. Please guide me in Your truth. Give me eyes to see You, a heart to be more like You and a boldness to follow in Your steps. Help me to love the unlovable. Help me to be patient with the hurting. Help me to bring peace and joy to those that are broken hearted. May they see more of You in my life and less of me.

Have you ever heard the sound of God's heart beat? I haven't but I think it has a sound like BOOM---BOOM---BOOM. It's steady. Never fast, never slow, but steady.

At 5am I open the door to a nice cool morning. Steam rolling off the pond. It's quiet, except for the occasional chirp from a bird in the neighbors tree. Beautiful. Just beautiful. The sun is peaking over the edge of the horizon. A new day has started. This day isn't like yesterday, it's new, it hasn't been used yet. My thoughts of an amazing God, a loving and living God, make me smile. What wonders will God accomplish today and who will He use to accomplish them? Me? You? The meanest person you know?

There is only one person who has truly heard the heart beat of God. His Son. But His heartbeat is evident in every moment of our lives. A birth, a death, a moment that takes your heart away. Maybe it's the quiet night sky, or the busy city street that He uses to catch your attention. He's big, He's mighty and He loves you. I don't know how to love like He does. It doesn't make sense to me. It isn't logical. All I know is I must trust him. I know that when it's over and I look back, I will see His hand all over it. I will see His heartbeat throughout every battle.

Jesus cared for His disciples. He loved all of them, even Judas. The Pharisees (religious leaders) had been trying to plan Jesus' arrest for quite awhile. They didn't like Jesus' explanation of God and His laws. They didn't like the thought that the laws weren't meant for paper, but for the heart. Then the greatest opportunity came to the Pharisees, Judas. The only way He could have been arrested was from the inside circle. By one of the twelve.

Why would someone so close to him turn on him? Jealousy? Greed? Who but Christ knows what turned Judas' heart towards betrayal.? Betrayal never comes from the outside, always from the inside. The one betrayed is always close to the one betraying. Crazy as it seems, I can imagine how it happened.

A ministry growing stronger every day. Everyone is included. Everyone feels important, everyone has a part, everyone focused on one goal then. It happens. My will, my goal. What's most important to me becomes my focus. Why doesn't everyone want to do it my way? Why is it his way or their way all the time? My way is better. What about me, what about my part? The betrayal begins with a simple battle of wills. My will against their will. My goal against their goal

God's will, His heartbeat, His goal, isn't like ours. It doesn't beat the same way. It doesn't skip or get out of rhythm. It doesn't get distracted. Jesus had a will and God had a will. Jesus gave up His will to follow his father's. My will, is different than my father's too. If I fight against it, turmoil, deception and then betrayal will come. I have become a betrayer. But if I make my will submit to His, then BOOM! I get to be a part of His will. I get to be a part of His goal, His heartbeat

Judas chose his own will, his own heartbeat over Jesus'. Jesus chose God's will over His own. Now what about you, what about me? Whose will are we going to choose today? Whose heartbeat are you going to follow? BOOM---BOOM---BOOM....

I have had to ask God many times to rescue me, heal me, give me strength, wisdom, understanding. I've had to repeatedly ask for forgiveness, grace and mercy. Satan wants me to think I am not brave. That I don't have what it takes to be a "real" believer. But he is a liar. In my own strength, He is right, but in Christ I can do all things. I can be brave today, strong in The Lord and in His mighty power. I won't let Satan fill my heart with fear. I won't let so called godly people lead me away from Christ. I will read Gods word and learn the truth. I will be bold in Christ, trust when He wants me to speak and to be still when He wants me to be still. I will be prayerful about everything. My attitude, my character, my thoughts, my dreams. I can't control anyone else's. God didn't give you or me a spirit of fear, but a spirit of love, peace and a sound mind. When Jesus looks at me, I want Him to be pleased and say "well done. You have fought the fight, you have kept the faith, you have finished the race."

Amazing how swiftly life has gone by, yet at the same time, how slowly it comes when you are waiting for something to happen. A vacation, a promotion, seeing a loved one come home, a birth, a miracle, a promise. The closer it gets the more excited you become. Everyday lasts longer than you want it to. You prepare for days and weeks for this moment.

Looking forward to something is the best anti depression therapy you can get. It gets your whole attention. Depression is often caused by not seeing beyond today and living on the unanswered promises and dying dreams of yesterday. Stop it. Don't do that. Yesterday is gone. God has given us a promise of peace, love, joy, etc., in this life in spite of our circumstances. Paul was in prison when he wrote encouraging letters to the believers and followers of Christ. He didn't enjoy being in prison, but he had joy. He wasn't in peaceful surroundings, but he had peace. Don't let the outside dictate how your inside feels. Let Christ saturate your every thought. Rely on Him to get you through. Read His word. It's life everlasting.

Faith, Hope and Love. Running into His presence to get strength for today. I don't have giant faith, but He gives me enough faith for today. My Hope is resting on His promises. And it's His love that holds it all together. It's not my faith in me, it's my faith in Him. It isn't my hope in this world, it's my hope for eternity. It isn't my love for Him, it's His love for me. I must decrease so that He may increase.

Battles are inevitable. Setting out to win them is a choice.

Remember The Lord Your God. This is a requirement not a suggestion or a question. It isn't an option. Do it or face the consequences. Gods people are required to remember Him. Isn't that a strange thing to say? That He has to command/require, someone who claims to be a part of God's people, to remember Him. But it's true. We forget him so easily. Things seem to distract us.

God warned the Israelites constantly. He did amazing things right before their eyes. His presence was a cloud by day and a fire by night, right in front of them. How could they forget him? It was easy. We do it all the time. Our eyes and our stomachs. Yes it's our eyes and bellies. They are never satisfied. They constantly want something, even if they don't need it. They forget to "Remember The Lord Our God". They forget all the miracles.

The Israelites complained constantly about their circumstances and blamed someone else for it. (Sound familiar) It was their own disobedience that caused it. They forgot how badly the world treated them, and wanted to go back to worldly misery. Why? Why do we do that? God told them about this awesome place He was taking them He provided everything for them, yet they weren't satisfied. They would choose a life of misery over a life of blessing. Isn't that what we do? Isn't that how we act?

I've read about the battles of Israel. God did some amazing things with them. Every enemy He delivered to them and they conquered. God has given us ways to defeat the greatest enemy of our lives, but we rarely use them. We aren't any different today than they were then. God has made us promises. He has given us a map and guidelines to follow to get there. He has delivered enemies into our hands and some we destroyed

Some? Be honest. We didn't destroy our enemy. We justified and kept the plunder. It's just (insert here). It's not bad. It reminds me of all the fun, the pain, etc. it's worth something. I can't just throw it away. What plunder, have you kept? What part of your life haven't you given to Him? What part of your life do you need to justify to prove to God it isn't bad? One reason Israel wanted to go back is they brought the "plunder" from their bondage with them.

They started bringing the enemies plunder, "the good stuff", back with them instead of destroying it. This "good stuff", created a web of deceit and they got tangled in it. They forgot to "Remember The Lord Our God". God's grace is amazing. But if you want to be free, He will set you as free only if you want to be set free. You have to let go of those things that weigh you down and make you forget. Pray, ask God what things are making you forget. They will probably be something you won't want to let go of. Remember The Lord Your God.

What would you do if someone you loved told you, "You are going to deny you even know me"? You love them. You've been their friend through horrible circumstances and through amazing victories. You know their secrets and have kept them. And now this. You feel betrayed. You feel hurt. Deny the one person you said you would die for? No way! Not gonna happen. Well it did. I denied Him, not just once, but multiple times. Why? Why would I do that to the one I love? Pride and fear. Yes, I could've stood up and said "Yes, He is my best friend, I love Him more than my own life." But that would have been a lie, wouldn't it?

Lies. Unintentional? Sometimes. Necessary? Probably not. But it ended with my broken heart and my betrayal. I hurt the one I love. He told me I would, but I denied that too. Denial and lies seem to go hand in hand. I'm glad He also told me He would still love me. My integrity was gone, my promises failed, my hopes and dreams shattered. I denied Him. Pride will make you say "I have never denied him." But how did I deny him? How did I claim to not know him? My life and how I live it every day. I say I trust Him. I say I love Him. I say all kinds of things. But when life gets dirty, or when life gets too blessed, I live my life the way I want to. Not the way He wants me to. I'm so thankful that His love for me doesn't depend on my love for Him.

Start your day, with this thought. Jesus really loves me. Jesus really does care about me. Jesus really does want my attention, my heart, my soul. No matter what my life has been before. Jesus loves me and He always will. And today I will not deny Him.

There was a man, he was rich and powerful. He had lot of friends, a lot of people that followed him where ever he went. He fought and won many battles. All he had to do was wait 7 days. In 7 days he would receive the biggest surprise of his life. Day 1, Day 2, Day 3, etc. Day 7 arrives. Now where is my surprise? Where is Samuel? He's bringing it. Meanwhile, the enemies were mad, they outnumbered him 100 to 1. At any moment they could attack. Each day was a struggle to stand strong. Each day was life and death. It didn't matter how great this man was, his enemy was greater. On day 7 he begins to think, maybe Samuel isn't coming. Maybe something happened to him, maybe he changed his mind. So this great man, decides to take matters in his own hands. He did what he thought was right, but only to find out it cost him everything. How many times has this happened to me? How many times, if I had just waited, if I had just been patient. (Patience has never been a strong trait of mine. It's a painful process, but I am learning.) Just like this great man, called King Saul, I have taken matters into my own hands. Saul didn't obey. If he had waited, his kingdom would have lasted forever. But instead, his Kingdom would come to a terrible end.

That's a pretty high price to pay for not obeying. You would have thought he would learn. You would think I would have too. Making mistakes is way too simple. Sometimes a mistake is a choice. Just like Saul, just like myself and you, we have decided to take things out of God's hands and do what we "think" God would want us to do. But all He wanted was for us to wait. To be patient, to be faithful, to obey. He was bringing the answer. Yep, how many times have I prayed and waited for just a little while, not even seven days, then try to answer my own prayer. Only to fail, and put not just myself in a poor circumstance, but my family

This wasn't the first time Saul disobeyed, nor was it the last time. In the end, God regretted making Saul king. Now that's the part that bothers me most, God regretted. How would I handle that? Knowing that because of my disobedience God regretted giving me something, putting me in a position at work, or at home.

I'm so glad Jesus died for me. I must never take His grace for granted. I must keep my eyes on Him, my heart pure and then learn to wait on Him. It isn't easy, but I've learned from some consequences that waiting on Him, would have been so much better. Pray and wait. Wait for your answer. You aren't God. Answering your own prayer is an act of disobedience. Repent and turn back to him. He's waiting, patiently.

Outside were conflicts, inside were fears. Nevertheless God, who comforts the downcast, comforted us. God sent Titus to Paul to comfort him, to encourage him. Obey God today. If He stirs your heart to say a kind word, an encouraging word, to someone, just say it. So many people are hurting not just physically and emotionally, but spiritually. We could be the hands and feet if God, if we would but let Him use us. Now to those who are hurting, put your stinking pride away and ask for help. Pride is the beginning of a great fall. Pride will cause you to fall down and not let anyone help you up. Accept help when help comes. You didn't receive help because you did not ask for help. You could be cheating someone out if a wonderful blessing.

We fight our personal battles within our own hearts and minds. We use our weapons to defeat the enemy, or the enemy defeats us. Some reasons I have lost are: I failed to fight. I gave up. I quit too early. It wasn't the right time. Others reasons could be I didn't know how to use my weapons or I just didn't use my weapons at all. Our enemy is always prepared and will use every weapon available to him. Hmm..... and we wonder why we lose.

We win some battles. We lose some battles. But when it comes to war, that's different. Wars are strategic. Winning this mountain is better than winning that hill. Winning a battle, or losing a battle, doesn't mean the war is over. We don't want to lose the war and neither does the enemy. It's a fierce and strategic battle after battle. We may be in a battle against depression, drugs or alcohol. We may be fighting against anger, bad attitudes, poor circumstances of life, a sickness or disease. We may be fighting to be first, most important, or wealthy. Maybe we think it's easier to just accept defeat. WE ARE ALL FIGHTING SOMETHING.

We are all in a war as well. This war involves everyone and everything, it is a war for souls. The most important war for all eternity. That's why Jesus came, isn't it? He helps us through battles, win or lose. But the real war is for our soul. The enemy wants it bad. He will do anything for it. But God wants it more. He gave everything for it. His Son. So fight your battles, don't quit. Whether you win or lose, don't quit. Start again, get prepared. Remember losing a battle, or winning a battle, doesn't mean it's over. It means, to regroup, re-dedicate, re-commit and fight again. I know in the end who wins the war and I want to be on the conquering side. I want many souls to enjoy eternity with Christ. Don't you?.

I often forget what God has done for me, only because I focus on the problems in front of me. Then He gently reminds me, He is here. I may be hit from every direction, but I will not be crushed. I may have to walk through very difficult days, but He will calm me and steady me. I may have needs, be in distress, be beaten, go through legal issues, or get exhausted and hungry, but He will never leave me. So I keep myself pure and increase my knowledge of Him. I will have to deal with a lot.

I must choose to be kind. To be lead and filled by His Holy Spirit. To love completely, and be honest, not by my power but by the power of God. I will not let lies (or truths) concerning me distract me. Everyone does not know me or my story, yet many do know my name. Each day I am dying and yet each day I am living a wonderful life.

Though I may have little, or nothing, I have everything. It is so good to know, through every trouble I have had and every trouble I will have, He will be there with me. He will calm me and let me know I am His and He loves me no matter what.

God's amazing love. It can show up and be felt at any moment. After Jesus died and rose from the dead, some of his friends were walking. A man joined them and began talking to them. Their hearts had been broken by the death of their Lord, but as they were walking and sharing about the last few years, this man began to speak. For a moment all they knew was He made them feel better. But when it was revealed to them who He was, the shouting began. Jesus will walk through every battle with us, every disappointment, and every broken heart to help us feel better. But it's not until He reveals himself to us personally, when you see who He is, that the shouting begins. Pray. Talk to Him and let Him reveal Himself to you and then let the shout arise.

It is never wrong to encourage someone. Encourage each other in The Lord. Remind each other of His love, His promises. Sometimes we all need encouraged. No matter the position or circumstance of life. Whether rich or poor. Whether we are sick or we are well. Whether we are a believer or a sinner. Jesus Loves us soooooooo much.

While we were in Chicago, we got stuck in traffic. I can say I didn't like that at all. After being raised where a traffic jam usually happens during harvest time behind a tractor, these people, do this every day, all day long. Traveling 4 miles can take an hour. What caused their traffic jam? Seemed to me everyone was going the same direction, at the same time. Lots of angry faces pushing, cutting in, trying to just get through, to get out. It was like a mass exodus. Fast cars could only go as fast as the old slow car in front of them.

How frustrating that must be. A car built for speed, idling still in traffic. I've felt that way, only I wasn't in a car. It was within my mind and in my heart. Feeling the need to run, but stopped by my own impossibilities. Grr. I know with God all things are possible, but that scripture doesn't do any good if we don't believe it. Now does it? Though Paul sat in chains, he was free. Though Peter arrested and in prison, he was free. It's the state of mind. A position of heart.

Can we be free, and still be bound? Yes. Circumstances of life can bind us, but we can still be free. It doesn't matter whether debt or sickness has you in its grips, or lack of education or too many degrees. It doesn't matter if prison or family life has you bound to a current position of life. Take heart. Jesus loves you. His freedom goes beyond who or where you are and takes you to where He is.

God has given me everything I need to live a life that will honor Him. He has not only given me the greatest gift ever (salvation with a promise of heaven), but He is giving me parts of his character, his nature. There are days I fail because I let my own character, my own nature, come thru. I know I need to add a lot things to my faith, scripture says to do your best to improve your faith by adding goodness, understanding, self-control, patience, devotion to God, concern for others, and love. If you keep growing in this way, it will show that what you know about our Lord Jesus Christ has made your lives useful and meaningful. (2 Peter 1:5-8)

Having a meaningful and useful life, is what we search for, isn't it? Stop expecting the world to give you anything that would make you think your life has meaning or that your life has been useful. The meaningful life the world wants you to have is full of guilt, disappointment and regrets. Spend some time with Jesus today. Honor Him with your life. If your life isn't honoring Him, then start today by asking for forgiveness. Stop behaving badly and honor God.

I've already lived long enough as someone who didn't know God. I've been immoral and followed my own evil desires. I lived a life of drinking and partying, worshipping my own idols, bowing down to my own gods. I have lived a life of a Pharisee. I have tried to please God by obeying rules, by doing what is right in the sight of men. I have tried to be a "Christian". But it kept me guilty and bound.

When I finally understood that Jesus really does love me, it changed my life. It's not that I can't do everything moral or immoral, it's that I don't want to. It's not that I have to obey Christ and follow His teachings, it's that I want to. Loving Jesus Christ is more than just reading His word. It's more than just following rules. It's so much more. It's a change of an attitude, a change of a heart. May you realize today the love of Christ has for you and for those around you, and may you find joy in it.

Today is Friday!! It's time to let the light shine. What happens when you walk into a dark room? At first you're disoriented, you stumble, trip, fall, or maybe you stand still, hoping that your eyes will get used to the darkness. If there is but a small glimmer of light, your eyes will find it. Your eyes will focus on it and use the tiniest bit of light to try to see. But what if there is no light? What if it is complete darkness? No glimmer, no reflection, nothing. What do you do? Search for a light? A light switch? A candle, a flashlight? You search for a light. We weren't made to be comfortable in darkness. Fear lives in darkness.

Do you see where this is going yet? You weren't meant to dwell in darkness and neither was I. We were created to dwell in the light! Our eyes were created to see, our ears were created to hear,

our mouths were created to speak. Right? Then why do we want
to sit in darkness? Why do we want to stay blind of the bad things
we do? Why do we want be deaf to the terrible things we say? If we
say we love God, then why don't we listen to him? God is light and
in Him there is no darkness. None! There are no shadows. There
is nothing but light. There is nothing but good. Nothing but truth.
   Have you ever been in a room with no shadows? It's bright.
There are lights everywhere. You can see everything. Every
wrinkle and every hair. Our eyes have a hard time adjusting to
such a bright light, but they do. We squint, blink a lot, our eyes
may water, but we focus. Sometimes it even hurts, but we adjust.
It's blinding to look directly at the light source, but that's what
our eyes are drawn too, isn't it? The source ? God is the source of
light in our lives. He reveals himself in such special ways. And
when He does our eyes (hearts) are drawn to him. It's what we
were created for. If you love Him and follow Him, then this bright
light lives in you. Those who are in darkness are either drawn to
you because they are lost and want to be found or your light repels
them because they don't want any part of knowing the truth. This
world needs Jesus. This world needs the light to chase away the
darkness, to remove all the shadows. Pray for boldness to let your
light shine. May the light of Jesus cast away all fear and darkness,
not just from your life, but from the lives around you too.

   Why do we take so lightly our salvation. Many have died
to share it. Many have given their life to carry it to the most
dangerous places in the world. Religious people from a longtime
ago, only heard about it but never got to be a part of it. Salvation
is something even angels from heaven want to experience. What
about it is so "unappealing" to some that they despise it, but
others are more than willing to give their life for it? It's cost is
immeasurable, yet it is so freely given that anyone can receive it.
Those who share it pay a high price so that those who receive it,

can receive it for free. Remember today is the day of salvation. Today is the day to share it. Share the love of Jesus. It's the only gift that truly keeps on giving.

Can you hold the oceans in your hand? Can you count the stars in the sky? Can you measure the width of the heavens? No, but Our God can. Your problems may be big, but they cannot be bigger than God. Some problems we have are the reaping of what we have sown. I don't like it either, but we were warned. That doesn't mean God can't or won't heal or deliver. But how much sweeter is the victory of those who have overcome? How much greater the celebration for those who have fought with God on their side and won? How bold and confident are those who have walked with God through certain destruction?

We cry too much over wrong choices. We are distracted too often by bad decisions. We blame everyone and everything else for our circumstances. Only a true man or woman can take the blame. Only a sincere heart can honestly say "I'm sorry, forgive me". Satan uses these things to weaken our spirits to the point of defeat. Don't let him defeat you. Take every request to God, take every care. He will understand and He will help. Remember, helping is not always bailing you out. But helping you is showing you the right way to walk thru it.

Yes you are unworthy. Yes you deserve every bad thing that could and has happened. No you are not good and you are not perfect. No one is good. Until you can admit that, you will never need a Savior. You will live a self righteous life. Then on the other side, we have those that believe they are too bad to be forgiven. Too evil, too far gone and have lead too long of a life to deserve a Savior. What's the difference? Nothing, both are lost.

I can't get to heaven without Christ. There is no other way. I can't be good enough, obey enough, to get there. No matter what good I have done in my life, it is not good enough to get to heaven without Christ. So I am in the same boat as everyone else. I need forgiven. Jesus came to give us life, to save our souls, to show us the way. It's time to trust Him and follow him. But how will you follow Him unless you know who He is? And how can you get to know Him? By reading His word, talking to Him and listening to Him.

There was a man sent from God whose name was John. This man came to bear witness to the Light. John was born with one purpose, and that purpose was revealing Christ. Preparing the hearts of men and women to see and accept the "Light". Have you ever thought that was your purpose? We have all been given the job by God to share His love with others. His love isn't rules and regulations. It isn't being chained to a church pew and it isn't looking down on others. His love was expressed through a cross. An evil torturing device used by evil men to cause pain. Jesus' love was expressed there for all to see.

So why do we express His love only when things are going well. His love for us poured out like water on the rocks beneath Him. His love for you began the moment you were knit together in your mother's womb and His love for you will never end. We can reveal Christ in every part of our life. The good days and the not so good days. Let the Light of His love shine through you. Show the same mercy and grace to others that Christ has shown to you.

There is so much going on that it is easy to let down your guard. It's easy to get tired. It's easy to "give-up" for just a little while. My bible says to "stand fast", which means be immovable, fixed, unshaken. To remain firmly standing. There are days that I become too tired to run, too tired to fight. I just get too tired of all that comes each day. My bible says to stand. We all have seasons of running free, basking in God's loving presence. But those seasons are usually before or after a battle. I've had battles that I was not prepared for and the damage was severe. I have wanted to give up and run. I have scars from those battles. They are there only to remind me to stay in His word, stay close to Him. If you are in a battle (as many of us are), stand fast. Put your foot on the word, grab hold of your battle gear and stand fast!

I got excited this morning when I realized today is my day to greet at church. I've been told I'm crazy, but I know where I come from. I'm still so amazed that God could accept me, little ole me, to share His love with others. So I'm practicing on you this morning, "Welcome to Little Chapel Church, I am so glad you came."

Come sit with your friends this morning and worship an amazing God. You may not think He is amazing yet, but give Him a chance. He knew everything about me, and forgave me. So to me, He is amazing. I doubt you would have forgiven me so quickly and so easily, had I done the things to you that I did to Him. Nope, I'm not perfect. Not even close and it still doesn't stop Him from loving me. Now, doesn't that give me a reason to smile? If you need a reason to smile, He loves you too, just where you are.

Each morning I can choose whether to wake up thanking God for all the things in my life or I can choose to complain about them. I can start my day on a good note or a bad note. I can thank God for my home, my family, my job or I can complain about them. Choose this day who you are going to serve. Jesus that died for you or Satan that steals, kills and destroys everything that you are. The choice should be easy, huh? By looking back on my day, it surprises me how often I serve the wrong one. So today, I choose to serve Jesus. To keep my eyes on Him and maybe at the end of today, I can look back and say, "good choice".

Lost, defeated, ridiculed, broken and beaten. Ever been there? Have you ever yelled "God where are you? I trusted You, where are you? I've told everyone I trust You. I've told everyone You will deliver me. Where are you? I am alone, everyone has left me. I have no one to turn to, no one to talk to, no one will help me. I remember You helped the others when they cried for You. Yet day and night I cry for You and all I get is silence. I'm weak, my strength to fight is gone and the world is about to crush me. Where are you?"

Have you been there, wondering? Asking the same things? I have. I have felt this way. Even now, but here is my hope. God hears me. He is listening. Because I know He is listening, I refuse to stop giving Him praise. Because He is listening I know that the end result will be His perfect will, not mine. Because He hears me, He will answer. His miracles are happening. Souls are being saved, families are joining back together, lives are being transformed. His blessings are being poured out. Because of this, I will praise Him. Because He loves me, I will praise Him. Because He is always with me, I will praise Him. Because He is God, I will praise Him. I will lift His name above all my troubles. And I know, in time, all my troubles will seem small compared to His greatness. So here is my life. Here is my soul. Here is all that I am. I am Yours and You are mine.

Today we can choose to be goats or sheep. There are two kinds of people. One is a sheep that depends on the shepherd. The other is a goat that does it own thing. One enjoys taking care of people while the other is selfish and cares only for itself. Today's is going to be HOT. Everyone will be hot and uncomfortable. Many will be short tempered, rude and impatient. But you be patient and be kind. Our shepherd will be where you are today and He is watching and caring for his sheep. Let Him decide who the sheep are and who the goats are. It's not your job, it's His. If you see someone that needs help, just help them. If you see someone working hard and you are able to give them a hand to lighten their load, then do it. If you see someone tired, take their place for a while. Make our Savior proud to call you his sheep otherwise you may fall into the goat category.

Ever wonder what it would have been like to walk the dirt roads or sail across the sea with Jesus? Would we get tired of walking, get scared when the soldiers came? Would we be astonished at the people who were healed and those that were not? Would we marvel at the people who were delivered from evil spirits and those that left with them? Would you be content to own nothing, yet have everything you need? What would we expect? Bread and fish at every meal? A storm every time we crossed the sea? Would we listen? Would we ask questions? Would we understand what Jesus was saying? Would we say the teachings were too hard and walk away.

I don't know everything. I don't understand much. I question a lot and have very few answers. All I know is that life is hard and with Jesus everything is possible.

How are you treating your relationship with Him? Are you forgetting? Are you distant? Have you left Him completely? Do you speak to Him daily and listen to Him direct you through your day? Do you realize that the only part of this relationship that has changed between you and Him is you. He doesn't change. He never has and He never will. And you wonder what happened?

Why your heart feels so distant from Him? He didn't move. His love didn't decrease. He didn't walk away. But you did. That's why your heart is troubled. That's why you can't sleep. That's why loneliness surrounds you even in the midst of a crowd. It's Him that you really want. It's Him that you really need. With Him all things are possible.

But you choose to live with the impossible. He is waiting for you, but sadly, He will not wait forever. We don't understand or comprehend "eternity", but He does. You are His desire and He loves you. Every wound, every drop of blood, every word He spoke was for you. It wasn't for the angels. It wasn't for the demons. It was for you. To give you the only opportunity you would ever have to become His for eternity.

So, what are you going to do? You can't just "fix it". You can't just "ignore it." You can't act as if nothing happened. True repentance and true forgiveness is the only way back. So stop walking away and turn around and face Him. He will forgive and heal a broken heart. I know, because He has forgiven mine.

Jesus' resurrection power is real. How do I know? I'm a witness to it. Are you? I once was dead. Not in body but in spirit. Then Jesus' love and power resurrected me. He gave me life. Have you been resurrected? If not, you may not be ALIVE!

Confession.. Lately I have not been praying as I should be and my attitude has been horrible. I am being reminded again how important prayer really is. If you are not praying, you are weak. Our prayers are life and death to ourselves and others. We are all called to a life of prayer. Though not all to the same capacity, we are all called to stand in the gap for each other. Families are being attacked and our response is? Our Christian brothers and sisters in other countries are being killed and our response is? Our nation is falling further and further away from the Word of God and our response is? The churches effectiveness towards the lost is seemingly still and our response is?

My prayer life must change. There are too many losing the fight against Satan. Not excluding the believers. If you don't have a prayer life, start one and start it now. Someone is in desperate need of it. Prayer isn't just asking for forgiveness, it's also talking to God on behalf of another person, place and need. Instead of complaining something isn't going your way, pray. God will change you or He will change the circumstance, but nothing will happen if you don't pray. Pray for your church leaders. Satan attacks them more than you could ever know.

We continuously under estimate the power of our God. Have we truly forgotten what He does to those who defy Him? Have we bowed down so much, that we have forgotten how to fight? Have we been defeated so much that we have forgotten the taste of victory? Today, remember who your God really is. He will not remain silent forever and He will remember those who are true to Him. Get your heart right with Him. Stop behaving as if He doesn't exist. Remember that He is the creator of all things. He holds in His hands. The deepest ocean and the highest mountain. Remember He loves you. Remember His son Jesus Christ. He came once before and He will come again. Remember and let it stir your heart to worship Him.

I haven't posted much lately. God has been reminding me how important prayer is. How important is it? When I spend time with God, I get more done in a day. Spending time with Him is not wasted. Spending time with Him prepares me for the day. Spending time with my Savior strengthens me for the challenges ahead, for the moments that can make or break me. Prayer can change things, and even when the things I need changed don't or the circumstances that surround me take me to my knees, I will be stronger because I spent time with my Lord.

I am not perfect. I lose control. I feel inadequate for all God is asking me to do. But my time spent with Him, whether it's 30 seconds or 12 hours, is needed and is worth it. My life is busy, just like yours. I have skipped a day or two from reading. I have skipped a day or two from prayer. I can feel it in my attitude, my temper, my lack of grace, my lack of mercy. I can feel it when I miss my time with Him. You can see it in my actions and in my words. When I don't spend time with Him, I become weak against the world. My Jesus knows me, whether I talk to Him or not. It is I who needs to get to know Him. It is me who needs His presence. It is me who needs this relationship with Him to be strong. "Jesus help those today that know you, to know you better. Help those that don't know you at all, to meet you."

Has your heart been hardened? Do you still not understand or perceive what He has done? He can do abundant things with the little that you have if you will give it to Him and allow Him to break it and share it. It doesn't matter where you are in your storm. Whether you are at the beginning, the middle, or the end. He sees your struggle. Sometimes when we seen Him it scares us. But if you listen closely you will hear "Don't be afraid, it's me. I'm here with you".

Today, for me, there needs to be a death so that I can walk among the living. I must die, so that Christ can live in me. It's Sunday. I've been busy all week. Busy with work, busy with caring for my family, busy with meetings, busy with things. You see life is busy. These things have drained me, discouraged me at times, and encouraged me in others. But it has emptied out every good thing in me. So today I'm going to celebrate my death and join the land of the living.

I'm not talking about my physical death, but the part of my life that is bringing death to it. Though my body isn't as strong as it has been in the past, my spirit is stronger than it has ever been. John said he must decrease so that Christ may increase. That is my prayer.

Fear is the absence of hope! This world will take all it can. It will try to destroy everything we work for, hinder everything it is able to. But my God is stronger, wiser, and more powerful than this world could ever dream of. This world doesn't have a hold on Him and the only hold it has on me are the things I won't let go of. The world may think it has control, but the world was not there when I was hidden away in my mother's womb. The world didn't create me. It can't heal me, deliver me, make me happy, or satisfy me. The world can arrest me, put me in prison, it can even lock me away and throw away the key. But it can't take my joy. It can't take my salvation and it can't take my hope. Those are things I would have to give up.

So now tell me again. Why do I let this world worry me? I look toward Heaven for that is where my hope comes from. I keep my eyes on Christ for that is where my strength is. I commit my heart to serving the Lord that is where my salvation is. This world is like a roaring lion that has been de-clawed and has no teeth. It sounds and looks scary. It may be big and it may stink. It could injury me or even kill me. But it can't take my soul. My soul belongs to the Lord.

Why would He want to talk to her? She's been married five times and is living with a man that isn't her husband. She's the scourge of the community. Why did He go out of His way just to talk to her? Why would He ask her for a drink of water? Doesn't He know she's filthy, she's nasty? Doesn't He know her reputation with men?

All I know is He didn't care. He didn't care what I thought about it. He didn't care what you thought about it. He didn't care what anyone thought about it. He loved her enough to stop and make time for her, a lost soul. He knew what her soul was worth. So whether it's you, someone you know or don't know, Jesus knows the worth of a soul. He died for it. Love God and love others.

I'm trying hard to remove myself and all my selfish feelings. It isn't about me. It is all about Him! It goes beyond just putting up with those I don't feel comfortable around. Those I don't agree with and it goes all the way to giving my life for them. That's Christ like. Only loving those that agree with me, those that are my biggest fans, those that are easy to love and get along with, is the easy way. It's not the Christ like way. He realized that everyone He met needed Him. He was their only hope. Once He finally gets that in my heart, then I will be the most Christ like. I can pray, I can teach, I can sing beautiful praise and worship songs. I can lay hands on those that are sick, deliver those with demons. But if I don't love like He does, then I am nothing. All my earthly recognition is worthless, pointless, a waste of time and breath, if I don't love you like He does.

Five loaves and two fish were not enough to feed all five thousand. Yet all five thousand were hungry. "You feed them" He said. We don't have enough, they got overwhelmed. Men in a fishing boat rowing hard against the wind, the storm was raging, it was dark. Yet they rowed and rowed. "Keep rowing" He said, "if you stop you will drown, you will be lost, keep moving." Jesus saw their need. One needed food for the belly, the other needed strength to believe. He saw them before the need ever presented itself as a need. He saw their desperation before it ever became fear.

"You feed them" He said. We can't was their reply. "You keep moving" He said. We can't they screamed in fear. Overwhelming circumstances easily distract us from seeing Jesus move in our lives. Our earthly needs quickly outweigh our earthly sources and we get overwhelmed. We aren't distracted by outside things, it's the inside things that get us. Fear, anger, jealously, etc. you know, the things you are dealing with right now, at this moment. I can't make it. I'm not good enough. I'm too busy. Too much, to handle. Where was their focus that day? Where is yours? Where is mine?

The things we can touch, the things that are temporary, catch our eyes and our hearts. But listen to Christ. He is saying "Don't look at those things. They will always be there. There will always be a need that needs met. Look to me. Focus on me. The things I will give you are eternal. I am the one who will meet your needs. I am the one that can calm your fears. I am the one you are seeking for. I am right here. I see you and if you believe in Me, you will see Me."

Jesus saw the hungry 5000 and fed them. Jesus saw the men in the boat and He got in the boat and calmed their storm.

Jesus loves you. He always will. But He hates your sin, detests it. It makes Him sick. Your sin will separate you from Him, forever. Today is the day of salvation. Today the Groom may come. Today could be the "Great Wedding Day". Choose for yourself today who you are going to serve. For me, I'm choosing Christ.

What if you were the only one called to spread Gods word where you live and where you work? What if the only prayer being prayed was yours? We have all been called to represent our

Lord and Savior while we walk this earth. How well have you been representing him? The disciples were just men. Just like us. Simple, hard working people. People that had families and jobs. Their love for Christ far outweighed the fear of men. They weren't super men or women. They were called and their calling from God, was greater than their fear of men. I need a closer walk with Him today than I had yesterday

There is only one who has loved me for a thousand years and will love me for a thousand more. He sees my tomorrow, He sees my today. He sees every bitter, every envious, every broken piece of my heart. He sees my hopes, my dreams and my desires. He sees my future and He knows my heart, He sees it and I can hide nothing from Him. He knows I love Him and He knows what stands between me and Him. He died just for a chance to rescue me. He encourages me to continue, to keep moving forward. He is the only one who could be my Savior.

No one else in all of Heaven, was pure enough or holy enough. No one else can go everywhere with me. No one else can understand me better. My husband, my family, my friends, can only go so far. They can only understand so much. They are limited. But my Jesus, He has no limits.

For you, He sees your broken heart too and understands. He has watched you struggle. He has seen your beginnings and He sees where you are right now. No matter how afraid you are, no matter how bad things may look, He is there. His name can cause a multitude of demons to flee. His presence can calm a raging sea. He can speak a word and create a life. Just a touch from Him can heal for an eternity. Trust Him when you feel you can trust no one. When you feel too overwhelmed and your desire is to quit, whisper His name, scream His name. He isn't too busy. He isn't slow. Because He is already there.

It is Sunday!! Where ya gonna go? Church? Yeah, I know, church isn't what saves you, but it sure helps make the week a little easier. I've gone to church most of my life. Notice I said "most". For a little while I wanted to skip church because I thought it wasn't important. That's when I knew more than my parents. I had began to do things that I now regret. I got the taste of the "free life". Church just seemed boring. It didn't have much to do with my own day to day life.

Then came the day that the emptiness was about to consume me. The guilt was about to kill the last ounce of joy I had and my broken heart was about to shatter into a million pieces. Why? I faked being happy. You can only do that for so long before it shows. I had no joy, no contentment, no purpose. Have you ever been there? Are you there now? For me the first step was searching for Jesus. I don't care where you find Him, because He is easy to find. Next step, talk to Him,. Ask him to forgive you for being the terrible person that you are. Yes, we are terrible people, not good people with issues.)

Then find a church. I don't care where you go, just find one that shares the gospel, the truth. Not one that tickles your ear, but one that steps on your toes. Not one that makes you feel all goody inside, but one that makes you want to be a better believer. We have enough clubs around here. We need more MASH units and battle stations. I'm fighting everyday and I get beat up a lot. I need strengthened and trained by my Savior and Commander Jesus Christ, Individually it's easy to lose battles but when we are in a group, a squad, we seem to win more. We don't have to stand alone. And when you know someone has your back, you are bolder and stronger. Go to church, find one. I have suggestions on where to go, but I'm not an advertising agency. Just a believer that loves Jesus.

Even a very small candle can light up a dark room. Hey, don't forget to talk to God today. He has something important He wants to tell you.

Ever wake up hungry? Not hungry for food, but for a spiritual filling. Hungry for a move of God. Hungry for His presence. I know that nothing else can satisfy that hunger in my soul except Jesus. So I'm beginning my day with some music. Then I'm going to jump into the middle of His word. When I search for Him, I will find Him. When I knock on His word, He will open it up to me. When I ask for His attention, He will give it to me. Are you hungry? Are you content where you are? Are you happy with your attitude, your thoughts, your spiritual side of life? This world can only satisfy for a moment, but my Jesus can satisfy for a lifetime. He gives me a drink that quenches my thirst. He gives me bread that gives me the strength I need for today. Ask, Seek and Knock. Got to go, He is waiting for me.

Started my morning off with a beautiful sunrise and reading Hebrews 11 & 12. The faithful ones who lived and died believing in the promises of God. Some lived crazy lives, some lived quiet lives. Some died of old age and others died very young. Some died with riches, while others died destitute. Yet all believed in the same God, the same resurrection, the same Heaven. They all looked forward to the same promises. They all counted it worth it, not giving up or giving in.

My name may not be listed next to Peter or Paul's name and it may not be written by David's or Samson's name. My name may not be on the same page as Mary's or Martha's or even Stephens name, but this I know. It is written in the same book. No matter where I am in this life, rich or poor, healthy or sick, I have a promise of a city with foundations built by God. The very same promise that every believer is offered today and every day. It's up to us to accept it, believe it, to have an inextinguishable faith in it. May God smile on you today, because you believe in Him.

Love never gives up. Love cares more for others than for self. Love doesn't want what it doesn't have. Love doesn't strut, have a swelled head nor does it force itself on others Love isn't always "me first", doesn't fly off the handle, doesn't keep score of the sins of others, or revel when others grovel. Love takes pleasure in the flowering of truth, puts up with anything and trusts God always. Love always looks for the best, never looks back, But keeps going to the end. If I can speak like an angel, if I can move mountains, if I give everything away to those who have nothing, if I give my life for what I believe, but I don't show love.... Then I am nothing.

Sometimes I find myself dragging my feet with sadness. Other times I have a angry, heavy step. Still there are other times I have a joyful and playful skip. My attitude may change from moment to moment. Sometimes I may seem focused at one task and distant at another. Whether my eyes be full of tears of joy or sorrow, my Savior never changes. He watches over me. Whether it is from a mountain top, or walking along side me. He knows at any moment He can make everything calm with just a word. He can calm me or He can calm my storm.

This is the part I am trying to learn... waiting. being patient, listening and knowing Him. Understanding that He is God. He is always fair, always true, always Holy and I am not. With His guidance I can be better, stronger and wiser. So I wait, listen, and follow.

Jesus loving me. Now, doesn't that give me a reason to smile? If you need a reason to smile......He loves you too. Right where you are.

During church, they brought in a woman who was barely dressed. The men dragged her all the way to the front of the church. Then they accused her, in front of everyone, of her crime. Everyone knew the punishment. So they all picked up their rocks. They all knew that the only verdict was guilty, the punishment was death. The man speaking bent over but never picked up His rock. I watched Him as He looked at the congregation holding their rocks. He knew the answer. So He stood up, looked at the woman and said to the congregation, "The ones of you who are sinless, you throw first, then the rest of you can finish it." Then He bent back over. I thought He too was looking for His rock, but He wasn't. He didn't have one.

One by one they dropped their rocks. One by one they stepped away and sat back down in their pews. Then I realized where I was, I wasn't the woman...... I looked down at my hand. I had a rock. "Oh dear God", I thought, "what have I become. These rocks are rocks of pride, not stone." The only way I could throw a rock was if I thought this person was less than me. The only way I could accuse someone to the point of punishment, was if I thought I was better than they were. I still hear in my ears, the words I have spoken against them for so many years. It is making me sick in my soul. I looked at the man speaking and said with tears in my eyes and a broken heart in my chest, "Forgive me". He said the same thing to me that He said to the woman. "Has no one condemned you? Then go and leave your life of sin."

I have discovered more in this story than I have ever noticed before. I have discovered that when I put someone down, when I get angry at them because of their sin or their situation in life, that I was attacking their worth before my Father in heaven. I discovered that I am the one standing right there accusing them with the stench of sin on my own hands, just like the Pharisee's with the adulteress woman. The only one who could have thrown the rock showed mercy and grace, love and compassion. The ones who were holding the rocks were full of self-righteousness. I once was blind and self-righteous. I once was deaf and self-righteous. I once was lame and self righteous. But praise God, now I see. God is revealing to me my own sins, my own rocks.

Many people have told the story. My parents had already chosen my future husband. That is how things were done in those days. We followed rules, memorized everything that the teachers taught us. It was required. Disobeying meant death. My dreams of getting married and having children was just a few months away. Then came the visit. I was afraid, yet his words calmed me instantly. "Chosen" He said. Me? I am nothing. Just a servant but He chose me. From that moment my thoughts were no longer filled with the wedding plans, but how to raise this child. It wasn't just any child, but it was His. My future husband, what will he think? Will he accept this news? The first child I bear, will not be his. The first child I will bear is destined to save the world.

My daughter was just barely a woman, her father and I had chosen a man for her. He was a carpenter and a good one. His father taught him how to make a good living. His father raised him to be a man, taught him how to protect and build a life with his own hands. My plans for her since her birth was to raise her to be a good wife and mother. It is how things are done. It is the only way things are accepted. Now this "visit" has changed everything. I don't know what to believe. All I know is now things will be difficult to explain. It was more than a visit, it was a promise fulfilled. Christ the Savior of the world enters the world through a womb.

The story began a long time ago..... the promise was given generations before. Some may think that this story ended on a cross or in a tomb. But I believe it is still going on....

The world needs to know Jesus loves them. How will they know if they are never told? God's grace is truly amazing. It can go deeper than any ocean. It can go higher than any star. God's grace will meet you wherever you are. No sin too small. No sin too big. All is forgivable in the eyes of our Heavenly Father.

What you decide today could change your future. Try looking beyond this moment. What do you see? Can you see the future or can you only speculate what it could be? We can only imagine what "could" happen in our future based on things that "have already" happened in our past. We base our future ideas and plans on things that have already happened. But God does not work that way. God does not base your future on your past. There is only ONE who knows your future and that future is not based on your past successes or your past failures. God knows everything about you. As amazing as it may seem, He loves you. He always has.

You may feel unloved and unneeded at this moment. You may feel like a burden or you may feel like you have been forgotten. You may feel nothing. No joy, no anger, no happiness, yet no sorrow. You feel numb to this world. It doesn't matter how you feel, right now, at this moment. God, your Father in Heaven, is telling you right now that He loves you. You are special to him. From the moment you were conceived, you were marked special. I know, "If He thought you were so special then why are you going through this?" That isn't a question I can answer except by saying......

Every battle, every war, each moment of peace, each moment of victory has brought you here, to this point in life. And here, at this moment, the Creator of everything wants to tell you, "I LOVE YOU and that what you decide today could change your future. It is your decision, no one else can make it for you".

Got hit square in the face this morning. Pray for your enemies. Bless those that curse you. Do good to those that use you. Give to those that ask and don't expect anything in return. Except that your Heavenly Father will take notice of you............ Jesus said it.

Knowing God is in control, makes today even better. Today someone's life will be changed. Someone will walk away from God believing that living a life for Him is too hard. While someone else will run towards God knowing life without Him has been too hard. Each day you are given the choice. You can choose to walk with him or walk away from Him. Choose wisely.

Sometimes our perspective, or the way we want to see things, is wrong. We are waiting for someone to have the answer for our economy. Someone to "right the wrongs". Someone to defend and protect. Someone with the cure for cancer, diseases, racism. Someone with the right words to say. The right things to do. Someone to show us the right way. We want, we say, someone to believe in. Someone we can trust. A few men and women are selected and placed on a ballot. A vote is cast and a decision is made. We have chosen. The one we chose made wrong decisions. Made wrong choices.

We forget they are human and we believe they failed. We should have known, right? There was a man who came in on a donkey. The people cast their vote and chose Him. Believing He was on His way to a kingly throne. But a few days later they believed He made a wrong decision. A wrong choice. He chose the temple and not the throne. He chose a cross and not a crown. Then He chose death and not a palace. They believed He was the "someone". And they figured He failed.

God's ways are not our ways. What man had planned would have been only temporary. What God planned was eternal. Things may not be going how you planned. But if you have chosen to do His will and not your own..... It may look like defeat right now, but real victory is coming.

When was the last time you committed your life to Jesus Christ? Committed to pray, to read his word, to live a disciplined life and to attend a church that preached the word of God. When was the last time that you followed through with it? We all have good intentions, but we don't like discipline. We pray on occasion. We read the word every now and then. We even attend church on holidays or days when life gets too rough. But when it comes to really committing our lives to him... that is going too far. When it comes to reading and praying every day, that just messes up our schedule. So be it!!!

Yes, you are not in a right relationship with Him.

Yes, you have let sin and worldly things become more important than God

Yes, you have caused heartache and disasters in your heart as well as in the hearts of others.

Yes, no one else may want you and no one else may want to forgive you.

Yes, you have sinned against God. But most importantly....

Yes, God still wants you, still loves you and still knows your name.

Yes, He still wants to forgive you.

Yes, He sent His son to take YOUR death sentence.

Yes, to pay for all the wrong things YOU have done in your life Yes, to pay for the sin YOU committed against Him.

Why? HE LOVES YOU. Open up your heart one more time and call out His name. It doesn't matter if it's a scream of desperation or a whisper from a broken heart. He will hear you. It's as simple as saying "God forgive me, the bad person, the one who has been wrong, the one who has blamed you and hated you." He will hear you, if you mean it, and He will mend your broken heart.

What? You want me to go tell them? They are horrible. You want me to go there? That place is huge and full of evil people. Ok, I will leave in the morning. You want me to leave now? God, I don't want to go talk to them. I hate them. They deserve every bad thing to happen to them. Don't you see how bad they are? Don't you see they are full of evil?....I'm not going. I will run far away in the opposite direction. I am going to put as much distance between me and that place, that person, as I can. I would rather die than go there. I would rather sleep for eternity than to tell them anything good to change their life.

Is that you?? Have you ever had those thoughts? Have you ever detested someone so much that you would rather die than to talk to them? Especially if what you are suppose to tell them could change their life.... for the better.......It has happened before and seems to continue happening. We get angry and feed our anger. Even to the point of death to our soul.......We get angry at God because something good happens to them. We cheer when bad things happens to them.

God asks, "Is it right for you to be angry? Is it right for you to be angry when I do good for them?" We give our justification to Him, but He says, "What part did you have in my creation? How much labor have you put in it? How much? None. You would rather die and spend eternity away from Me, than to give a person another chance to get things right with Me? It is not your call. It is mine. Don't ever forget that."

Our anger gets the best of us sometimes. Even to the point of disobeying God and running from Him. Stop feeding the anger and start praying for them. Forgive them. This world needs Jesus. You may even save your own soul from destruction.

Believe and keep believing.
Live and keep living.
Love and keep loving.

To Abby,

I will love you forever. I'll like you for always. As long as I'm living my baby you will be. 9 lbs and 10 oz when you were born. You began walking at 9 months old. Climbing to the top of the kitchen cabinets before your first birthday. You have always wanted to do everything your sisters were doing, no matter their age or what they were doing. Which led to many, many fights. You are your own person. Special in every way.

You are a born leader and a natural athlete. Smart and kind. I see the compassion you have for others and the passion for the things you love doing. You are more like your dad than you will ever know and he will ever admit. You are strong and full of courage. You will do things and say things that others won't and because of that they won't always like you. (Just ask your dad.) Don't let this world confuse you. Don't let people your age dictate what you like or don't like. The one wish I have for you is more of Jesus in your life. You are/can be a life changer. Every struggle you have today, will prepare you for the struggles of tomorrow... IF you will learn from them. Listen to the wisdom of the old people. I failed to do that. Chase your dreams. Don't let anyone try to stop you. Do you remember your dreams? You have such a big life in front of you. Let God be a big part of it. The biggest part hasn't even started yet. You know right from wrong. So do what's right.

You know the good things from the bad things, so do good things. I bless you Abby, from my heart and from my soul, on this day, your 17th birthday. May God bless you with Godly wisdom, Godly understanding and with Godly knowledge. May He fill your life with hope, faith and love. May He guide your steps, light your path and restore everything satan has taken from you. May your smile be full of joy, even on the bad days. May peace fill your mind and follow you everywhere you go. May your days be full and your nights restful. May you feel the love of Jesus every day. You are amazing now, and I am so excited to see what God is going to do with you next.

Love Mom

To Sadie Michelle Steed,

I love you. I remember your smile when you were little and your love of wearing hats at Granny's PaPa's house. I remember your little curls. I really thought your hair would be like mine. Those bright blue eyes, that saw everything. I remember you. I remember your care for the other children who had a booboo. I remember you riding your rocking horse as hard and as fast as you could. I remember you cheerleading, your gymnastics (I always thought you were pretty awesome at them).

I remember watching you run track and for the first time ever watching you triple jump at State.. I remember you. I remember your 5th birthday party. The greatest puppy party ever. I remember when you lost your first tooth. I remember when you cut your hair to get gum out. I remember you. I remember your love of children, especially those who were blessed with special needs. I remember your patience, your kindness, you love and your joy. I remember you.

I know you, I know you are precious to me, to your dad and most important precious to Jesus. I know you have the ability to see everything and want to make things right. I know you have the ability to make others smile, when you are hurting inside, that you have the ability to make others feel beautiful. I know you rarely complain about the things you don't have or the things you didn't get, or the places you haven't gotten to go. I know you are amazing. I know you are an amazing worker, when you set your mind to it. I know you can do anything, but usually set back and watch others do it before you. I know you don't like sitting in the middle, but would rather be in front on in back. I know you and I love you.

I don't have a lot of money to give you or to buy you expensive things. But I can give you this, my heart and Jesus. It is the greatest gifts I can give you. My heart can do nothing but love you and want great and amazing things for you. But it is Jesus that is the most amazing gift of all. Every dream you have had, every heart's desire you have felt you can get through Him. He is the best thing I can give you. He will be your friend when you are lonely, He will be your healer, when you are sick. He will be the one to comfort you, when sadness comes. Jesus will be the one to guide you through life's obstacles, through dry places and places in your life that seem too difficult.

Jesus will be the one who can open your eyes to the amazing things He has for you. Jesus will be the one who will walk every day of your life with you. I love you my sweet Sadie, when the days get dark and scary always know your mom loves you and even better and most important Jesus loves you too. When the days are bright and cheery, when things are going your way, remember your mom loves you and even better Jesus loves you even more.

Love Mom

Happy Birthday Corrina!!

I love you more than you know. This day 20 years ago you turned me into a mommy for the first time. You have taught me so much over the years. Just like Myah will teach you.

So train her up in the word of God. Not just by words from your mouth, but by the works of your hands. Be the best wife I know you can be. Support the man God has put in your life. Remember you don't always have to prove your right. Love unconditionally. Don't keep score of rights or wrongs. Encourage those around you, even if they don't deserve it. Be the first to ask for forgiveness and the first to forgive. It makes life a lot sweeter. Go the extra mile. Take the extra step for those that you love and even those you don't know. I wish I could buy you many wonderful gifts.... but silver and gold, I have none. But what I can give you is "Jesus".

Love Mom

Printed in the United States
By Bookmasters